Life Is Beautiful: Live It Right!

Published by
Gita Publishing House
Sadhu Vaswani Mission,
10, Sadhu Vaswani Path, Pune – 411 001, (India).
gph@sadhuvaswani.org

© J.P. Vaswani
First Published – 3000 copies – December, 2020

LIFE IS BEAUTIFUL: LIVE IT RIGHT!
ISBN 978-93-86004-26-0

No part of this book may be reproduced or utilized in any form or by any means, electronic or mechanical including photocopying, recording or by any information storage and retrieval system, without permission in writing from the Author.

Printed by
Thomson Press (I) Limited

Life is Beautiful: Live it Right!

J.P. VASWANI

Compiled by
Dr. (Mrs.) Prabha Sampath
and
Krishna Kumari

GITA PUBLISHING HOUSE
PUNE, (INDIA).
www.dadavaswanisbooks.org

CONTENTS

	Compilers' Note	7
Chapter 1:	The Sacrament of Marriage	9
Chapter 2:	The Joy of Parenting	37
Chapter 3:	Karma	72
Chapter 4:	Spirituality In Daily Life	117
Chapter 5:	Conquering Fear	140
Chapter 6:	Gateways to Heaven	166
Chapter 7:	Death is not the End	192

Compilers' Note

Anyone who has ever sought Dada's advice, or had the opportunity to place before him a question that has long troubled them will vouch for this truth: Dada's attitude to life is refreshingly different – it is not that of the preacher who dogmatizes, nor that of the stern moralist who pontificates. He is a saint who loves his fellow human beings, and his love and understanding blended with his wisdom, gives him a unique insight into men and matters, life and its complexities. Truly, he is the ideal teacher who elucidates, explains, enlightens and above all, inspires.

In thousands of informal and formal talks and discourses, in hundreds of books and numerous Question-Answer sessions, Dada has tackled the shocks and griefs, the pains and problems which trouble us all. No issue is too abstract, no problem is too facile for him to dismiss. If you go to him with troubles or difficulties, he always responds meaningfully, constructively; and he always makes a difference! His understanding of human nature is deep; his readings of the world's great books and scriptures is wide; and his knowledge of the testament of life is profound. But all this is made accessible to the least amongst us, by virtue of his love, his profound sagacity and his wonderful ability to express the most intricate truths in the simplest words. Each and everyone of us, from the very young to the very old, from the uncomplicated to the most convoluted thinkers, can drink at the ever flowing fount of love and wisdom that his words offer. No wonder then, that every subject he touches upon, is deeply illumined and made satisfyingly accessible to us all.

And let us add, there is hardly any aspect of our lives that Dada has left untouched by his enlightened discourses! From marriage to parenthood, from prosperity to misfortune, from management to spirituality, from happiness to irritation, from suffering to death, there is no shade of life, no dark corner of the human heart that Dada has not illumined for our benefit. His books give us the distilled wisdom of his own tremendous intellect and his open minded, non-judgmental understanding of human nature.

When Beloved Dada's Centenary Celebrations were being planned, one of Dada's devotees expressed the wish that he would like to bring out a 'Digest' of one hundred of Dada's best selling books, in the form of a condensed compendium, so that Dada's insights may be made available to a new generation of youngsters who need to rediscover the art of reading. Beloved Dada himself approved of the suggestion, adding that whatever he knew, whatever he spoke and whatever he shared with us, was what he had learnt at the lotus feet of his Master, Gurudev Sadhu Vaswani. If the Master's message and his teachings were going to reach more people through such a compendium, he was all for it!

And so we are happy to place in your hands, the first volume of this collection – a condensed version – of Dada's most popular books, condensed with great care and effort so that the original contents are brought to you without any loss of their intrinsic value.

"Life can be changed. Life must be changed," Dada asserted firmly. In this collection, he shows us the way to transform our life into a beautiful journey to God.

THE SACRAMENT OF MARRIAGE

THE SACRAMENT OF MARRIAGE

Let me begin with this beautiful story from the Mahabharata, which tells us about the significance and sanctity of the sacrament of marriage.

A *tapasvi*, after years of austere penance to conquer the senses, was seated under a tree performing his daily rituals, when a dropping from a bird sitting atop the tree stunned him. His power was so intense that merely by gazing at the bird in anger, he burnt it down to ashes. The death of the bird saddened him but his own power surprised him and he felt egotistical and superior having acquired such control with his *tapasya*.

He was an ascetic who lived on alms and he went out to beg for food every day. He was used to women rushing out to touch his feet, bow down before him and seek his blessings, offering him the best, the choicest food from their homes.

This day was different. On reaching a home for *bhiksha* (alms), he was surprised by a request from the lady of the house, which seemed pretty legitimate to him at that point in time. The lady, with great respect asked him to wait for alms while she served her husband first. The *tapasvi* waited for a while but soon became angry and restless, having had to wait. He thought to himself, "Who does she think she is, serving her husband first – who is he anyway?"

His arrogance took the better of him as he addressed the woman, "Look, woman! I have asked you for food and I want it now, because I have no time to waste! I have devoted myself to the Lord and I lead a life of renunciation. It is the duty of a *grihasti* like you to provide me with food. Obviously, you are ignorant of the spiritual power of a *tapasvi*. It can burn you to cinders if you are not careful!"

The woman continued nonchalantly with her work and after

finishing what she was doing came out with food for him and calmly spoke to him, "O *tapasvi*, I did not keep you waiting without good reason. I was only doing my ordained duty, serving my husband with love and devotion. Your anger does you little good. I know you caused a little bird to be burnt to ashes just a while ago. But I am not like that poor bird!"

The *tapasvi* was stunned by the realisation that she knew all about him, even though she was just an ordinary housewife, according to him. He fell at her feet, "Thank you mother, for enlightening me," he said. "I have a lot more to learn about life and the world. I now know that the path you walk as a *grihasti* is as great and valuable as the path I have trod as an ascetic!" So true!

- Self-realisation can be attained by following the path of marriage and parenthood, by living in the world while treading on the path of love and service, of seeking and attaining.

- Marriage is a great institution that helps to teach and establish the values and ideals that will contribute to a good society.

- Couples who create a home where peace and serenity prevail, deserve to be credited with great achievement. When children grow up in an atmosphere of love and joy and imbibe good values, these homes contribute to the future of society.

- When married love matures, it becomes familial love; as familial love evolves, it grows further to encompass the society and community.

- In its final fulfilment, it achieves the capacity to love all – all people, all creation, all creatures that breathe the breath of life. When we become capable of such selfless, unconditional, undemanding love, surely we have reached the highest state of consciousness!

MARRIAGE TRANSCENDS MERE ROMANCE

In India, man and woman represent two aspects of the divine – as portrayed in the dual deity *Ardhanarishwar*. It is believed that the female is an equal, indispensable aspect of human life. Thus, there is no question of inferiority or superiority. Physically, emotionally, temperamentally, men and women are undoubtedly different. But one is incomplete without the other and they are equals in all aspects.

Marriage is a commitment for life. It is a permanent, lifelong relationship based on mutual trust and understanding. The ideal Hindu marriage insists that the newly married couple should work together for the welfare of the family.

Success in marriage is much more than finding the right person. I find myself rather amused when I hear young people talk about finding Mr. Right or Miss Right and the 'chemistry' that will ignite a spark when they come across the 'right' person. Love must not be confounded with physical sensation or sexual attraction. These are not enough to make a marriage successful. In marriage, being the right person is far more important than finding the right person.

Marriage is much more than a love affair based on mutual passion or physical attraction. Such a love affair only promotes selfish pleasure. When this pleasure wears thin, cracks begin to appear and the marriage begins to fall apart.

Marriage is not just an institution, it is a sacrament, a sacred union. It was after centuries of experience that the sages of ancient times formulated the rules of marriage. Just as there are traffic laws, which have to be followed to avoid accidents, similarly there are laws of marriage, to make wedded life happy, rewarding and successful. When you get married, your life is regulated by certain rules. Freedom (in marriage) is not doing what you like. Freedom is the ability to do what you ought to do and should do.

FINDING THE RIGHT PARTNER

If a marriage is to last a lifetime and be successful in every sense of the word, it must be based on harmony which does not depend on how one looks or how much money one has. It is the nature and the temperament of the partners that matter. And we have to make an effort to understand our partner!

A girl came to me and said, "There is this boy whom I wish to marry." "Tell me about him," I said. "He belongs to an aristocratic family," she said. "That is zero," I said. "He holds a doctorate in computer science." "Another zero," I said. "He is the only son, the only child of his parents." "Yet another zero," I said. "He is so handsome," she continued. "One more zero," I said. The zeros went on multiplying until finally, she said, "He is a man with sterling qualities of character and faith in God." "If that is so," I said to her, "then put one in front of all the zeroes and he will score that many marks." You must study the temperament of the individual and see how far your temperaments will be in harmony with each other. This is what will make a marriage last.

- Your emotional involvement with a person colours your judgement. The best people in that case are the parents to help you decide your future partner. They have the foresight and the experience to know who would make the best partner for you.
- Marriages are made in Heaven and it is our karma that decides who we are going to marry and who our parents are going to be and when and where we will die.

- Man and woman are a part of a whole, they can't survive by themselves. They complete each other. If men have the strength, determination, energy, vigour and guts, women have great sensitivity, spiritual aspirations, and the spirit of sympathy, service, and sacrifice. Men rely on their intellect. Women have intuition.
- Love may begin with physical attraction between the couples but marriage, in due course, fuses them together so that they form one complete whole. This is the purpose of marriage. When we forget it, we lose the proper perspective of marriage.

SECRETS OF A HARMONIOUS MARRIAGE

Most people believe that making money is the best way to ensure a successful marriage. Both men and women fall prey to this fallacy – for it is indeed a false belief to imagine that money can ensure happiness in marriage.

I met a wealthy man who complained to me, "I work hard day and night to provide my family with all the comforts that they need. I have risen to the top of the business world, and I am No. 1 in my sector. My wife has been given everything a woman could wish for, my children go to the best schools and have their every whim and fancy satisfied. Yet they do not appreciate all that I do for them. Tell me, what more can I do for them?"

His wife and children had a ready answer to that question, "Spend more time with us!"

A happy marriage requires:

- Love
- Commitment
- Understanding
- Patience
- Forgiveness

Both partners must enter into the sanctified relationship appreciating its great potential and its deep significance, knowing that they have chosen to live together, to bring out the best in each other, and to make each other as happy as possible.

Young people must enter into marriage with a serious sense of commitment, integrating head and heart.

Marriage is a commitment one makes for a lifetime which is not to be taken lightly. When you enter marriage with this sense of commitment, your home is sure to become a temple of love, peace, joy, and harmony – a center of light amidst the encircling darkness. The love and peace that emanates from such homes reaches out and radiates towards others. The parents and children from these homes have the wonderful ability to love and serve others, and can become the catalysts who transform society.

We all know that there is, there can be no such thing as a trouble-free marriage. Life brings its share of crisis, problems and challenges to every one of us. But what sees couples through all this is LOVE. Love which is selfless and can withstand the most severe of tests like financial loss and unexpected illnesses. Marriage teaches us mutual respect, mutual love, understanding, tolerance, and a sense of responsibility. Marriage disciplines us, as we learn to be selfless and put others first. Ultimately, love changes us for the better.

Do you know what the miracle of marriage is? It is two people who do not take each other for granted, but do take it for granted that they will love and cherish each other all their lives, and give that love priority over everything else in their life. Anybody can laugh together, but a loving husband and wife can cry together.

A happily married woman who celebrated her sixtieth wedding anniversary said to a writer who was interviewing her, "Nobody can find love if they go looking for it alone."

Love is not out there somewhere. It is with you, within you. You and your partner can make it flourish in your marriage. A miracle marriage is within the grasp of all couples who wish to give and take, understand, love, forgive, care, and share. Your wish for the miracle of lasting love can come true when you enter married life in this spirit.

A learned man I know once expressed the opinion that men and women too, should be required to undergo special training before they are allowed to enter marriage and parenthood. They should be emotionally, psychologically, and spiritually educated to make their marriages meaningful and enlightened. Human relationships flounder when mutual respect is lacking. Marriages fail when companionship and understanding are absent in the partners. Therefore, I urge husbands to respect their wives, and wives to respect their husbands. Children should respect parents and parents should respect their children's individuality and independence. Give each other the freedom to be themselves, to express themselves, and assert their unique identity! When there is complete understanding, respect and affection, all marriages become love marriages in the true sense of the word. But don't wait for the other to begin the process. Don't sit back and say, "How wonderful it would be if my wife grew in the spirit of understanding!" or "I wish my husband would cultivate the spirit of forgiveness!" Instead, begin with yourself! After all, if you don't change yourself, you can't expect to change the rest of the world!

A FEW TIPS ON HARMONY IN MARRIAGE

1. Do not argue about inferiority and superiority. Husbands and wives must recognise they are equal partners. There must be a congenial environment in the home in which each partner enjoys mutual freedom to evolve.

2. Make your married life, an offering to the Lord Himself.

Whatever it is you may be doing – teaching a child, helping him with his homework, attending to household chores, balancing the budget, or attending to guests – let it be done as an act of worship to God, in the spirit of fulfilling your *swadharma* (the duty allotted to you).

3. Learn to recognise God in each other. The ancient scriptures tell us, "Where women are worshipped, there the Gods rejoice." Unfortunately, many men accept this in theory, while in practice, they continue to exploit and degrade their wives. Instead, when we cherish the reverence for the soul, we will create an atmosphere of ideal love – a love that is strong in giving, sharing, and self-sacrifice; a love that is not threatened by the many accidents and incidents of life; a love that burns bright even in adversity; a love that shines as an ever bright lamp to guide us through the dark nights of life. When you worship the God in each other you lay a strong and secure foundation for a happy and harmonious marriage.

4. According to Hindu *dharma*, marriage is indissoluble. Make a few compromises, sacrifices, if necessary, to nourish your marriage. When mutual adjustments are made with love, understanding, and adaptability, your relationship will be smooth, stable, and enduring.

5. Always remain loyal, truthful and faithful to one another; I do not condone 'free' marriages where partners allow each other to do as they please. I must insist that sexual fidelity is vital to preserve the spiritual well-being of your marriage.

6. Realise that every situation, every predicament you face in your marriage is helping you to achieve your goal of self-realisation. When your partner displeases you, you grow in the virtue of patience. When you encounter disappointments, you imbibe the spirit of acceptance.

When an offence is committed against you, you grow in the spirit of forgiveness.

7. Do not deceive yourself with the false notion that you would have been better off married to someone else! No matter what kind of a person your spouse is, remember there is a divine plan, a divine meaning behind your union. With spiritual insight and love, you can bring about a tremendous transformation in one another!

8. Adapt and adjust. Develop the wonderful qualities of tolerance and flexibility. A little spirit of give and take can bring you great rewards.

9. Avoid negative feelings. Do not imagine the worst. Sri Ramakrishna once narrated a parable about a man who was lying on the roadside. A thief passed by and thought to himself, "He tried to rob someone and was beaten up." A drunkard passed by, and he concluded that the man had too much to drink. A saint passed by and thought, "The man has attained a state of identification with the spirit – and has lost body-consciousness!" Your imagination can mislead you. When your husband does not smile at you, do not conclude that he has stopped loving you. If your wife seems preoccupied, do not jump to the conclusion that she is simply ignoring you. If you have a little argument or misunderstanding, do not decide that your marriage is at an end!

10. Realise that your children are your greatest responsibility. Do not pamper or indulge them mindlessly. Blend firmness with affection, discipline with love, to give them a secure and healthy environment where they might grow to absorb the deeper values of life.

According to ancient Hindu scriptures, an ideal family should have the following qualities:

1. *Aashavaad* (optimism): When family members develop faith in God, they have no need to fear the unknown. They can look to the future with confidence and joy, for they know that God's Will is being done in their lives. The unknown and the unexpected will not daunt them, for they know they can turn every situation to spiritual advantage.

2. *Pratiksha* (patient waiting): When you have done your duty well, you can rest assured in the conviction that success will be yours. When you imbibe the virtue of perseverance, you will know that the divine hand is always holding you, and guiding you. You will be free from impatience and restlessness.

3. *Su-sangata* (good company): Learn to cultivate the company of good friends, well-wishers, and wise ones. Avoid contact with those who are likely to bring harmful influences into your family. Let me also urge you friends, to cultivate the habit of family *satsang*. Invite your relations and neighbours too, to join you in *kirtan*, *bhajans*, and recitations from the scriptures.

4. *Sukarma* (right action): Perform acts of charity and service. These do not have to always depend on cash and material offerings. Give of yourself. Spread kindness and cheer and optimism wherever you go. You and your family will be richly blessed for it!

5. *Atitthya* (hospitality): Hindu scriptures tell us, *Atithi devo bhava*. Our guests are manifestations of the divine. Welcome visitors to your home with warmth. Greet them cordially and offer them your best hospitality. The Gods smile at you as the guests depart from your home in contentment.

TEN COMMANDMENTS FOR A BLISSFUL MARRIAGE

1. AVOID QUARRELLING

Patience Is The Name Of Game: If one of you is losing your patience, the other should try to keep quiet, wait for the 'storm' to pass. Sit the other person down after the storm has passed and talk things over. Try to understand things from the other's perspective.

There were two people. They celebrated their Golden Anniversary. They said that in all the 50 years that they spent together, they had quarrelled not even once with each other – though both of them were known to have irascible temperaments. They both had the tendency to be angry at the least excuse. They were asked the secret and they said, "The secret is a simple one. When we married, we made a pact with each other that both of us would never lose our temper at the same time. We resolved that if one of us got angry, the other one would be patient. We have held on to that agreement through these 50 years and that is why our marriage has been such a happy one."

Accept Your Differences: There was a saint whose wife was short-tempered and querulous. No matter what he said or did, there were daily battles in the home. However, the saint took it all in his stride. "God be praised for giving me such a wife," he would say. "She is a constant source of inspiration to me to cultivate the spirit of *vairagya* (dispassion) in my heart. I don't even have to go to a guru to learn it. I can get it right here in my own home!" All of us hate disagreement and dissension. But they are inevitable in any human relationship. When we disagree – or agree to differ, as the euphemism goes – we are expressing our individuality and independence.

How boring the world would be if all of us thought alike! These differences must be cherished and accepted as opportunities to learn more and more about your spouse – and, in the process, reach a better understanding of yourself.

Forgive And Forget: Two men who had gone to the same school, met at a bar. They were delighted to renew their friendship and were reliving their past memories. Time fled, until one man realised that it was close to midnight. "It's been wonderful meeting you my friend," he said, getting up to leave rather reluctantly. "I wish I could stay on – but I'd better go home soon or my wife will get historical." "Historical?" said the friend, puzzled. "Don't you mean hysterical?" "No, I meant historical," laughed the other. "She will go back into the past, delve into the annals of our marriage and recount all my past mistakes and failings."

A razor-sharp memory is a very good thing – but not when it is used to carry around memories of past wrongs.

Yield More Than Resist: My advice to young couples is that they can handle frustration and pressure better, by yielding rather than resisting. When you become rigid and inflexible, you insist on seeing things as only black or white. This hampers mutual understanding, and isolates you in your hardened stance. After all, giving in does not imply giving up. When you yield a little, you will gain, more than you ever dreamt!

Compromise: One has to realise that nobody is perfect. We all have our share of unpleasant quirks, foibles, and eccentricities. An important part of marriage is to understand and make allowances for the failings of your partner. Every marriage will have its share of misunderstandings and differences. But the wise learn from them. You will find that you grow in emotional strength, wisdom and maturity. As one philosopher has said, "Adversity not only draws people together, but brings forth that beautiful inward friendship, just as the cold winter forms ice figures on window panes, which the warmth of the sun may efface."

2. BE A GOOD LISTENER

Listen to what the other person has to say. We like to talk but are not prepared to listen. Let us be good listeners. Of a couple it was said, "There was a time when he talked and she listened. On their honeymoon, she talked and he listened. Now that they are settled down in their own home, both talk and the neighbours listen."

Very often, one partner in a marriage has legitimate grievances, but the other is complaining too loudly to listen. Marriage can thrive only on a two-way communication! "She's always talking and I do nothing but listen," some husbands claim. I would like to tell them that they must distinguish between hearing, listening, and effective listening. Listening involves both hearing and paying attention.

When you fail to listen to your spouse, you cause pain and unhappiness – this leads to loneliness, alienation, hurt, and wasted moments of precious life. Concern for the feelings and emotional well-being of your spouse will surely prompt you to change your listening habits, for you hear best when you love! But I urge you to:

1. Listen to your spouse carefully.
2. Listen to your spouse's full story.
3. Listen to your spouse's full story first – before you react.

3. APPRECIATE YOUR SPOUSE

All of us yearn to be appreciated. All of us love to receive compliments, which assure us that we are loved and appreciated. When you express your appreciation of your spouse, you recognise their strengths, support them in the best way possible and make them happy! Actually, it is not very difficult to offer an honest compliment; each of us has many positive qualities.

When you take the trouble to identify these 'positives' in your spouse and compliment them on it, you will not only make them happy, but you will also build up their self-esteem. All it takes is a little sympathy, understanding, kindness, and a flair for the right words – and you can express your appreciation in style!

A middle-aged couple were attending a party. The wife was persuaded to sing a song. She sang so well that the guests gave her a standing ovation. Taken aback by the response to his wife's song, the husband blurted out, "I did not know that she could sing so well!" If your spouse has a special talent or gift, encourage her, appreciate her. Participate in her interests; allow her to grow.

Nowadays both partners work outside the home. Both are pursuing careers and living hectic, professional lives. It is even more important that they should take time out to talk to each other, share their feelings and express their appreciation for each other. This sense of understanding and appreciation should grow with time, so that the bonds of marriage are nourished and strengthened.

4. KEEP YOUR LOVE FRESH

After marriage, spouses take each other for granted. Women have complained to me, "There was a time when our husbands gave us many promises, made many vows, took great interest in what we did. All that has become a part of history. Now they take us for granted." Therefore, keep your love fresh. Emotional and physical independence come easily to men and women these days. I think there is something valuable about a relationship where husband and wife need each other, and are vulnerable without the other's support.

Take a good look at some of the following expressions:

"I am proud of you!"

"You make me feel good!"

"I love to be seen with you."

"My confidence gets a boost when you are with me."

"You have the ability to make me feel great!"

"Your sense of humour is terrific. I love it when you make me laugh!"

"I am so glad you are watching over me. I don't make mistakes when you are around!"

"Thank you for being you!"

And of course the seven-word magic formula, "Honey, where would I be without you?" In every one of the above expressions is the underlying message – I love you! You make me feel happy and secure. This is the secret of keeping married love fresh – permanently!

5. ACCEPT IMPERFECTIONS

No man or woman is ever perfect. Marriage involves the coming together of two imperfect human beings. Accept your spouse for what he or she is, not for what he or she would be, could be, or should be.

How do you achieve a blessed union?

The answer is simple: through selfless love. Selfless love seeks to understand, accept, sympathise, forgive, and appreciate. Selfish love, on the other hand, makes demands and nourishes impossible expectations. I am afraid young people today expect too much from married life. They look for material comfort, complete fulfilment, and a sense of achievement. Happy marriages are based on the principle of give and take. One of the fundamental requirements of a successful marriage is to accept your partner with love and understanding – to learn to live and love selflessly. Marriages are not meant to be magical tricks. Peace and contentment and happiness of the heart are not handed to you on a platter as a wedding present from God. You have to work to earn them.

When you adopt a realistic and compassionate approach to life and people, you will grow in understanding and maturity and your marriage can become truly rewarding. I know some people who pride themselves on being 'perfectionists'. I appreciate them as long as they aim for perfection in all that they say and do. But when they begin to demand perfection (as per their standards) from their partners, they are only asking for trouble!

Have you heard of the old saying, "A watched kettle never boils?" When we are constantly looking for something to happen, the very act of constant expectation seems to delay the awaited event! So too in marriage, when you keep an eagerly expectant eye on the partner, you are doomed to disappointment. I would urge you to train those eagle eyes on yourself instead and try to become the perfect partner yourself. When you adopt a critical judgmental attitude, there is the danger of the relationship being stunted and suffocated. Love cannot flourish under the critical gaze! Do not expect or demand perfection of your spouse. Even a word, a gesture, a wrong tone of voice can cause friction in marriage.

6. FORGIVE EASILY

To make marriage a success, to make it a source of happiness and harmony, you have to forgive much. It is the prerogative of marriage to give and give and give – and forgive – and never be tired of giving and forgiving. "How many times shall I forgive?" asked a husband. "Shall I forgive 7 times?" "No," came the answer, "You must forgive 70 times 7!" 70 times 7 is 490 times which means you must forgive without counting. And a wife complained, "I have been forgiving until I can forgive no longer. I have forgiven and received nothing in return." And she was told: "Continue to forgive without expecting anything in return." Forgiveness is the characteristic trait of selfless, unconditional love. It has rightly been described as the 'emotional disarmament' in marriage.

Forgiveness is not logical or methodical. It must be spontaneous. It is simple and straightforward – you accept your spouse's shortcomings and you continue to love.

As I have said repeatedly, no human being is perfect. Therefore, no marriage is perfect either. Misunderstandings, accidents, and quarrels will inevitably occur in any relationship. These may be over in a flash, but then, bitter memories linger. Some of us forgive easily, but cannot forget. And this is not enough. Therefore, I urge you to erase the bitter memories of the past so that your happy future may not be clouded. An honest apology, a generous acknowledgement, and loving forgiveness – that is all it takes to wipe out the bitterness and anger.

When you forgive with all sincerity and good faith, you can make a fresh beginning and pursue the possibility of "living happily ever after."

Of a great English poet, I read that he never spoke a word of appreciation to his wife. So long as she lived, he criticised her, found fault with many things she did. Suddenly, the wife died.

The poet exclaimed, "Ah, if only you had given me some notice, I would have written poem after poem in your praise, and expressed my heart's gratitude for all that you did for me!"

We value people only when they are gone. We place wreaths on their bodies and pay glowing tributes to them at memorial meetings. Let us do something for our dear ones, while they are still alive.

Keep your love fresh, but do not be attached to anyone. Attachment is the root of sorrow. No one belongs to you: You belong to the Lord. Therein lies the secret of the art of living. Alone you came into this world: alone, you will leave it. In the mid period, give as much love as you can to those that cross the pathways of your life. Give love to all, and forgive the wrongs done to you. Give love to all, seeking no revenge for offences and insults.

7. BE PATIENT, LOVING, UNDERSTANDING, KIND AND TRUE TO EACH OTHER!

I am afraid many of us have a rather shallow and superficial conception of love and marriage. We look upon love as something romantic – a thing of the heart. We regard it as something intangible, ephemeral, something which we can't even find words to describe.

If love is to grow and endure, it must be constantly nourished by understanding, shared experiences, sympathy, patience, and compassion. Such love is powerful – it has the power to heal, unite, enrich, and restore.

"What is the best way to understand?" someone asked me.

I could only reply, "The best way to understand is to be understanding."

Did you know that the word understand is actually related to its literal meaning – i.e., stand under something? Understanding helps you to grow in the spirit of humility. Stand under – stand under! Unfortunately, no one is prepared to stand under anyone else today. Everyone wants to stand above everyone else – no wonder then, that the divorce rate is increasing, and our homes are breaking! Parents say they cannot understand their children; children claim they cannot understand their parents.

Humility and understanding are the keys to harmony and happiness. When you learn to love and respect your spouse, when you begin to appreciate his/her special qualities, then your marriage bonds are strengthened. I am often disappointed and grieved when married men or women use the word "my" instead of "our". How often do people not say, "my car", "my house", "my son", "my daughter", "my bank account", etc. What is the purpose of marriage if you can't begin to substitute *us* for *me*, *ours* for *mine*? We must work constantly to remove egotism and materialism from love.

I would call for empathy among married partners. Empathy is nothing but understanding the other person's point of view. The golden command do-as-you-would-be-done-by is a splendid instance of empathy. It is an excellent technique for strengthening marriage bonds.

Tolerance is a great virtue in this age of individuality and self-assertion. Tolerance is nothing but the sincere effort to understand, appreciate, and respect your partner's beliefs and habits. This does not mean you simply accept the other's point of view. It only means that you make an effort to understand it!

True love enhances; it does not degrade or devalue. True love builds up the spouse's self-respect and does not diminish it in any way. If you truly love someone how can you belittle that person?

A happy and healthy relationship requires that you should give each other the space and time you both need to be on your own. It is both possible and desirable that within the framework of marriage, the partners should be able to maintain their individuality and creativity. This does not just mean having large rooms for your exclusive use where you can paint or sing. After all, how many of us live in mansions? What I mean by space is really the freedom and the opportunity to pursue those interests which your spouse does not share.

Tina and Pravin are a devoted couple. Tina is energetic, fun-loving and a live-wire, taking interest in all that goes on around her. She is a member of the PTA in her son's school, and the cultural secretary of their housing society and all these activities keep her busy and occupied. Pravin is a devout and pious man who calls himself a "practical businessman and an avid tennis player." His mornings in the home are sacrosanct. He likes to perform a traditional *pooja*, and includes the recitation of different mantras each day of the week. Tina and Pravin give each other the space – the time and the freedom – to pursue those activities that matter to them. And they are proud of each other.

Guru Arjan Dev tells us in the sacred *Sukhmani Sahib* there is a lamb and a lion within each one of us. Each rose has its share of thorns, amidst which the sublimely beautiful flower blooms. I think this symbolises the human predicament too. Understanding is the most precious quality a human being can possess. It cultivates your inner vision; it enhances the intuitive faculty which enables you to perceive the truth about yourself, others and your life.

8. HAVE A SENSE OF HUMOUR

If two people have to live with each other, they must learn to laugh and make each other laugh. We must laugh *with* others, never laugh *at* others. If we have to laugh at somebody, we must laugh at ourselves. Laughter is at once a physical, mental, and spiritual tonic. A husband, in the presence of his wife, complained to a friend, "There was a time when my wife used to bring my shoes and my dog used to bark. Now things have reversed. My shoe is brought by my dog, and my wife barks." The wife had a good sense of humour and she immediately said to her husband, "Why are you complaining? You get both the things right. You get the shoes and also the bark!"

It was a wise man who said that love can grow strong and healthy when it is nourished by the ability to laugh. Unfortunately, married couples seem to be losing the ability to laugh with each other, or indeed laugh at themselves. The world seems to have grown very serious nowadays. We tend to take life too solemnly.

We have even begun to equate maturity with seriousness. We believe that wisdom cannot be accompanied by laughter.

I would like to tell my married friends – it is a sad day, an incomplete day in your life, if you have not laughed together heartily at least thrice!

There is a little child in all of us who never ever grows old – no matter what our age. He needs to be coaxed to come out and play. True, life is a serious business and requires our deliberate consideration and thoughtful response. But a little fun and laughter now and then does plenty of good for everyone!

It is also said that before marriage a man yearns for a woman. However, after the marriage the 'y' is silent. I would say to the wives – make your husbands laugh, and you will have deserved every penny he earns!

Humour is an all-round tonic: It promotes your physical, mental, and emotional well-being. A woman once said to me, "My husband and I have been married for twelve months, but in all this time, he has smiled at me only three times!" Surely, that was a marriage which needed the all-round tonic of humour! Laughter diffuses stress and tension. It promotes relationships and improves communication. It firms up the bonding between you and your spouse.

9. IF THERE IS MISUNDERSTANDING, CLEAR IT!

Do not hesitate in discussing whatever is in your heart freely and without fear.

Many people have grown up in families where there was constant quarrelling and arguments. I dare say underneath all the noise and strife, these families really loved each other; but the trouble was that they only knew how to express anger – not how to express love. As a result, children of these families grew up thinking that expressing anger was also a way of expressing love. Yelling and shouting had become part of their psyche. Equally, there are others who grew up thinking that anger was meant to be suppressed. It had never been expressed in their families. There are safe and appropriate ways to express anger in a loving relationship. It has been said that anger is an opportunity to know yourself better.

It is argued that the healthy flow of love and affection in a marriage is controlled by the nature and frequency of the communication between husband and wife. Communication that has been withheld or postponed or suppressed during the day can be conveyed at night, and all misunderstandings cleared up. This will enable you to go to sleep in a happy frame of mind. When you communicate effectively and constructively, you can resolve issues much more satisfactorily.

It is vital in a happy marriage, for both partners to accept each other as *equals*. Marriage is a wonderful bond of companionship where no partner has to feel inferior or superior. If you do not treat your partner as an equal – beware, there is something wrong with your attitude! Love, understanding, and mutual respect are the fundamentals of a happy marriage – and that exists only among equals.

If you wish to eliminate misunderstandings, if you wish to grow in the spirit of understanding and appreciation – talk, communicate effectively – but do not argue! Let your disagreements never become heated or violent. When you are emotionally overwrought you raise your voice, you condemn the other person, you lose your temper – and a bitter fight is bound to ensue.

But we are human, and disagreements and misunderstandings are bound to occur. Be quick to soothe and heal the wounds and rebuild your sense of understanding and commitment by keeping the channels of communication open.

It is alright to allow your partner to express his anger, if only you can remain calm and tolerant in the process. If each of you does it in turn, ego clashes can be eliminated from your marriage. The truth is, arguments do not ever lead to amicable conclusions. Discussion, on the other hand will help you understand and appreciate the other's point of view.

You don't have to agree on everything – but you don't have to argue all the time, either. It is far more civilised to talk things over; and it takes maturity and wisdom to appreciate the other person's point of view.

Let me also add – you must know yourself well, before you communicate effectively with your partner. It has been said, "Two people begin to fight when they do not understand each other's language." What is referred to here is not the language of voice and words – but the language of the heart, love. Know yourself. Assess your own strengths and weaknesses before you judge another person!

Try to eliminate from your marriage all those negative tendencies which detract from love! Stop judging, stop accusing the other. Take joy in knowing your partner better. If you learn to understand, learn to accept your spouse, your children, and your family members, your marriage will truly be transformed into a wonderful relationship.

One of the most unfortunate 'developments' in the modern age is that the all-pervasive spirit of competition has even managed to enter the sacred sphere of marriage. I do not wish to say much about men's or women's liberation, but it is tragic if they are allowed to divide marriages. Marriage is for giving, not for taking. We cannot demand anything from our families – you are there to love them and serve them, and not the other way round. If you are a husband, I urge you to be devoted to your wife. If you are a wife, I entreat you to love and cherish your husband. You are both meant to be custodians and caretakers of the children!

10. COUNT YOUR BLESSINGS

Happy marriages are not handed over to anyone on a platter. You have to work hard at it – but God can give you all the help and inspiration that you need! According to our ancient Hindu ideals, the husband worships *Devi* (goddess) Herself in his wife. So too, the wife worships God in her husband. Both worship God in the child. When you imbibe this ideal, you become conscious that God is within each one of us, and you love and serve God when you cherish the members of your family. As you can see, this is a way of elevating human relationships, and making marriage and family life a means of moving towards God. This is indeed the greatest spiritual goal of the *grihastha ashrama*.

Let God be the focus of your home. Surrender yourselves to God, put your problems and difficulties before Him. Seek guidance from Him – not only in adversity, but at all times. The Hindu epics and *puranas* offer us a glorious and inspiring vision of the ideal marriage. Who can fail to be inspired by the story of Ram and Sita? Who would not be moved by the story of Savitri and Satyavan? How many valuable lessons may we learn from the story of Nala and Damayanti? These blessed couples were indeed ideals, embodiments of perfection – but we can always emulate their example to the extent we can! Loyalty, selflessness, fidelity, constancy, understanding, and patience are all wonderful qualities and these are the true ornaments of marital love.

In marriage, you must seek to be the ideal, dedicated partner, a companion to your spouse in spiritual evolution. When a married couple lose sight of this high ideal, their marriage can be nothing more than a convenient arrangement. Any marriage that does not rise above motivations of physical desire, social advancement and financial considerations will become merely a bondage.

I urge you to behold God in your spouses – offer love and respect and affection to them. Appreciate all that they are and all that they do. Fulfil your duties and responsibilities in the marriage and be an ideal companion to your partner.

PARENTS' ATTITUDE TO MARRIED CHILDREN

For parents, I would offer the following suggestions: Learn to let go of your children when they marry. They are entering into a new relationship, a crucial phase of their life, just as you did all those years ago. They are now acquiring new identities; they will now have to make their own decisions. You must learn to stop telling them what to do.

When your son/daughter speaks well of the spouse, do not resent it or become envious of the newcomer. Look for something to praise him/her and make your child happy!

Appreciate the new situation that emerges – a triangular situation between you, your child, and his spouse. It is far more complex, and you must deal with it in a way that will strengthen the bonds of love.

'In-laws are not outlaws,' as one perceptive marriage counsellor remarks. They are ordinary people like you and me, linked up together in a relationship that is both complicated and demanding, when their sons and daughters choose to marry someone else's daughters and sons!

Forging new bonds, creating new relationships, is not an easy task. But a little understanding and sensitivity can go a long way to establish loving ties within the extended family. Try not to become hypercritical or judgmental. Above all, keep your communication channels open!

THE GREAT VALUE OF *GRIHASTHA ASHRAMA*

The *grihastha* is one who lives in a *griha* or home. It is a household. Sri Ramakrishna attached great importance to marriage and home. When people asked him diffidently if *grihasta* could attain liberation, his answer was simple, "Why can you not attain God? He is the *Antaryami* – the inner ruler who is within each one of us. Think of Him constantly in your daily life as you do your work. You will find that He will take care of you!"

You may wonder why and when a home become a prison? It becomes a real prison when the people living in it restrict their lives, confine their minds to "I" and "Mine." "Get rid of I and Mine." When we are trapped in this narrow circle of egoism and selfishness, we lose the sense of the vastness and magnificence of the universe of which we are a part. We lose the sense of dignity and responsibility that is attached to the great *grihastha ashrama*.

- To be a true *grihastha* one must cherish the institution of marriage, and develop confidence and self-reliance.
- Stop constantly devaluing yourselves by saying, "I am only a *grihastha*. I am only a *sansaari* – I am tied down by my bonds." No! Cast aside such doubts, strengthen your mind, and broaden your vision.
- Vow to contribute to the betterment of your culture, your community, your society, your country, and the world you live in! This is your prerogative as a *grihastha*, a true citizen!

Sri Ramakrishna said to us: Live in *sansara* (the world), but don't allow *sansara* (worldliness) to live in you. He gives us the example of the boat and urges that the boat must be in the waters – but the water must not be in the boat else the boat will sink and we all will be drowned.

The new *grihasthas* of the new millennium can learn from the saint of Dakshineshwar how to make their married life glorious – by working together as enlightened citizens in a spirit of love and service.

It saddens me when a woman comments that she is just a housewife. That she is not a career women and confined to the four walls of the home. She does not know her real dignity and worth! If only she discovers her onerous duties and responsibilities as a builder of the home, as the shaper of a new generation, as the architect of a new India, she would not refer to herself in such belittling terms!

Let me stress, being attuned to God, being devoted to the spiritual goals does not mean neglecting your spouses and their needs and concerns!

Rather I urge you to behold God in your spouse – offer love and respect and affection to them. Appreciate all that they are and all that they do. Fulfil your duties and responsibilities in the marriage and be an ideal companion to your partner.

Harness God's power to your marriage and you will lack nothing!

THE JOY OF PARENTING

YOUR CHILDREN ARE YOUR TREASURE AND TRUE WEALTH

My Beloved Gurudev, Sadhu Vaswani, had wonderful things to say about the child and the child heart:

> The child is still a mystery to me. Does God come in the little ones to teach our hard and wayward hearts?
>
> Children come with radiant faces and singing hearts. Do they not come to renew the child-heart that slumbers still in the grown-up ones? Mystery-filled are the children, and radiant are they as stars. They come as witnesses to our unseen homes. In the eyes of a child floweth eternity: and in the heart of a child is the light that heals! Philosophers have evolved systems and built up schools. But I know of no better touchstone for truth and falsehood than the child-heart!
>
> Riches and glories of the earth pass away: but in the pure eyes and lisping words of a child may lie hidden, the wisdom that abides.

How eloquent and how significant!

In my *yatras* to the East and West, I meet several old, well-known friends; and I make several new friends, too. They are indeed wonderful people, and many of them are doing great things, achieving success in different spheres of human activity. Yet others are struggling, working hard to achieve the same kind of success, with varying results. Almost all of them are busy amassing wealth!

I would like to make it clear that I do not regard the pursuit of wealth as something wrong or immoral.

The point I wish to make is this: by all means accumulate wealth; but in the process, do not neglect your richest treasure – your children.

How careful we are about our investments! We study the stocks and shares before we choose what we think are right for us! My only question to you is this: are you investing enough time and attention on your children, who represent your real wealth? Rabindranath Tagore said, "Every child comes with a message that God is not yet discouraged of man." Children represent the hope, the future, the possibility of salvation for all humanity. As the poet Carl Sandburg put it so beautifully, "A child is God's opinion that the world should go on."

That treasure that God has placed in your hands – your child – is greater than all your assets, all your investments and all your diamonds and gold!

Give your children the love and attention they deserve. Money is not enough! Toys and games, fashionable, branded clothes and an expensive school are not all that a child needs. He needs your love, friendship, care, guidance and discipline. He needs his parent's loving attention so that he has the assurance that he is not alone, that there is someone who loves him dearly, someone whom he can turn to any time he wants.

The nature of the soul is love – and without love, no child can grow in the right way. You must give children your time! You must try to sow in their plastic minds seeds of character, without which life can have no meaning or value. You must help them to grow in the love and devotion of God.

I recall the story of a young man in France. Having committed a heinous crime, he was sentenced to hard labour for ten years. He received his sentence calmly.

But as he was being led away by the police, he turned towards the people present in court and shouted aloud so that everyone could hear him: "I have nothing against the judges – for they have dealt with me justly. I have nothing against the police – for they have done their duty. However, I can never forgive two people in this courtroom – my father and my mother!" People listened to him, shocked beyond words, too stunned to react.

"They are responsible for my present condition," he continued. "They paid no attention to my upbringing, did not take care of the company I moved in; they never bothered to find out who my friends were. True, they gave me money to spend – but did not bother to find out what I spent it on. They did not object when I gambled, took to drinking and visited houses of ill-repute. And so here I am – full of vice and crime. The fault is theirs but I pay the price for it, sentenced to hard labor in prison, to be branded as a convict for life!"

Harsh words! But the young man's bitterness cloaks the truth that many parents do not seem to comprehend their responsibilities towards children.

WHAT CHILDREN NEED

Parents are often overwhelmed by a sense of awe, wonder, mystery and deep love, when a new born baby comes into their lives. And at that time the thought arises in the mind of everyone – I am witnessing the miracle of God's creation!

In the Hindu way of life, love and care for the child begins even when it is in the womb. Hindus strongly believe that the mother's state of mind, her living environment and her spiritual attitude during her pregnancy influences the child in the womb.

It is very essential for parents to understand the various stages of development of a child, right from the time of his birth onwards. It is a human being who is being molded, shaped by them, even as they themselves evolve as mature, responsible parents.

Children live in the now; they are free from the anxieties of the past or fears of the future. If your child demands your attention, give it to him then and there; don't give him an appointment for tomorrow or later!

Never, ever let your child feel unwanted. Never forget, too, that every child is a unique individual, with his own personality and innate talents.

Understand him, encourage him to express his creative potential. Guide him in a healthy, constructive way, to bring out the best in him.

Keep your child very close to yourself, until he is at least three years of age. He needs the affectionate touch of his mother and the loving smile of his father. It is a great blunder to hand little children over to the care of *ayahs* or babysitters.

It is absolutely essential for mothers to breastfeed their new born children. I am well aware that many mothers today do not want to do this, for reasons of their own. The milk that is produced in the mother's breast is the property of the infant – not the property of the mother. The mother who refrains from giving her milk to the child is actually stealing what belongs to the infant.

Parents must learn to give unselfishly, ceaselessly, unconditionally to the little one who depends on them for his very existence.

Every child that God sends out onto this earth comes with infinite promise of love and joy and hope. But it can be realised, this promise fulfilled, only through love. This will make him live a good life and love you in return.

HOW TO BE A GOOD PARENT

You need not spend every living and waking moment with

your children – but when you cannot be with them, continue to communicate your love and affection to them and ensure that they understand that your business and profits are not more important to you than they are.

May I offer you a few practical suggestions on this aspect?

1) Spend time with your children:

Carry them around when they are infants; touch them, baby talk to them, tickle them; run around with your toddlers; play hide-and-seek with your youngsters; take them out to parks, gardens, zoos and the seaside; spend holidays with them; teach them computer skills and car driving as they grow older; be responsive to their evolving abilities and skills and make every activity with them an enjoyable game!

2) Treasure every important event of their growing up years:

Collect photographs of the children at every stage of life; keep their art-work, their projects and their drawings safely preserved. On a birthday or other special days, sit down with the child and go through your collection – and the happy memories attached to it.

3) Involve the child in your activities:

The seven-year olds in Class III were asked to write a paragraph on the most exciting day they had spent that year. Some wrote about *Deepavali*, some about the trip to the amusement park; little Tina wrote of the day she had spent with her dad, clearing the weeds from the garden and planting new seedlings. For her, it was "prime time" spent with her father – an unforgettable experience.

Take your child with you if you like to go for a quiet drive in the late evenings. If you like to watch the sunset from your terrace, keep your child by your side when you do it.

4) Give each child individual attention:

Rajeev's overseas business partner was invited over for dinner. The burly American was delighted to meet Pinky, Rajeev's eight-year old daughter. "Hello, young lady," he beamed. "Which class are you in?" "She's in class III now," Rajeev intercepted. Pinky's face fell; and the smile disappeared from her eyes.

Her papa did not remember that she had been promoted just two months ago, and that she was now a 'big' girl in class IV!

A teacher gave her class a sentence completion exercise to do. They had to complete the sentence beginning: "For me, happiness is..."

Nine-year-old Helen wrote: "For me, happiness is getting my feet wet on the seashore with mom – nobody else, but mom and me."

Devoting individual attention to a child is not always easy, especially when families are large, or when children are born too close to each other. But it's possible, with a little adjustment and lots of imagination!

The Kelkars have three growing children, Vishal(6), Varsha(5) and Varun(3). Every morning, it is papa's duty to get Vishal ready for school, and mama's, to see to Varsha. Varun is enlisted to help by being given important tasks like fetching didi's shoes and tasting dada's milk to ensure that there is sugar in it. If the parents are stressed or tensed about the day ahead, it is not communicated to the children.

Everything is put on hold until Vishal and Varsha are safely seen off in the school bus. Then mama tells Varun, "Now we can relax, while papa gets ready for work."

Find time to talk to each child about his/her day; listen to them carefully as they narrate their 'adventures' at school; at all times make them feel that each one of them is the light-of-your-life, the apple-of-your-eyes.

5) Surprise them with the unusual and the unexpected:

By this, I do not mean just gifts. All I suggest is don't let routine activities overwhelm your life. Don't get into ruts, doing the same things over and over again.

On Karan's tenth birthday, his father took him rowing at the local Boat Club, for the first time. Karan could never forget that day! He resolved that he would do exactly the same thing on his son's tenth birthday!

When your child asks, "Daddy, can I play with the garden hose?" or "Mummy, can I bake my own cake?" Don't come out with the stock "No!" For a change, say, "Why not?" And you will have made his/her day!

6) Communicate with your child:

Talk – listen – respond with understanding – express appreciation – show your disapproval. Whatever you do, however busy you may be, communicate with your child.

When your child nudges you, when he wants to talk to you urgently, stop whatever you are doing and listen to him with full attention.

The son of a famous writer was caught red handed, stealing from his friend's locker, in a prestigious boarding school. "You have brought shame upon your father," the Headmaster said to the boy sadly, when the boy was brought to him. "What will your father say when he hears about this shocking incident?"

The boy's voice quivered with emotion. "I know what he would say, 'Not now son, later!' This is what he always used to say to me whenever I went to him with a question or a bit of news – 'Not now son, I really haven't got time now. Come to me later.'

Why should he say anything different now?"

So, listen to your child – but listen gently, kindly, and lovingly. I know a family which has a large bowl on the dinner table: it is the 'Talk-about-it' bowl. Each day, the children put in objects or drawings or clippings into it, about which they would like to talk during dinner. Each one enjoys having his/her turn to talk at the table, while the rest of the family listens.

Do not neglect to express your negative feelings: when a child says, "I want to run away," or "I don't like you," tell him/her, "I think you must be really angry." When they have been naughty or careless, tell them, "Mummy is very upset with you for leaving your room in a mess."

A contrite, "I'm so sorry!" or a soft "Mummy loves you!" is enough to smooth ruffled feelings, and all will end happily!

7) Offer possibilities to your child:

Do not limit their world and restrict their options. Read aloud to them when they are young; give them books to read – and you open up endless hours of delight. Play music for them and initiate them into the joys of appreciating one of life's finest pleasures.

As a parenting expert put it so beautifully, "Open doors for your child. They may not want to walk through every door you open. But just keep opening new doors and allow them to enter wherever they chose."

"Remember," he continues, "love does not spoil a child; too little discipline spoils a child. Love does not mean fostering dependence; or allowing wrongdoing; or showering a child with gifts; or bribing him with rewards to do what he must do; love means building a child's sense of self-esteem."

PARENTS AS ROLE MODELS

"The mother and the father are the deities whom we know first and foremost," proclaims a well-known Tamil proverb. *Matru devo bhava, pitru devo bhava* – your parents are the equivalent of Gods, the *Vedas* emphasise. This is indeed a great honour! But this honour is to be earned, not just taken for granted!

Parents are not only their children's first and foremost teachers: they are also the children's role models and mentors. If you want your child to be exceptional, you must also become exemplary role models. As we all know, children are great imitators. They are extremely observant, attentive and sharp. In order to live wholesome, harmonious, meaningful lives, there are several virtues that we must inculcate in our children – virtues such as patience, tolerance, compassion, forgiveness and understanding. These virtues cannot be imbibed through sermons or lectures – but when they see you practising them, the children will adopt them readily and willingly.

Little Rohan's parents engaged the services of a young girl to look after him. The girl's name was Sangeeta, and she had been sent out from the village to earn a little money to support her impoverished family. Rohan's parents treated Sangeeta very harshly.

They constantly scolded her and berated her; they criticised everything she did; When Rohan entered kindergarten, his teacher was horrified to hear the language he used with his friends. "You stupid, clumsy fool!" he would yell. "Don't just stand there! Make yourself useful!" It was exactly the kind of language that his parents used to speak to Sangeeta!

IT IS NEVER TOO EARLY TO START INCULCATING VALUES IN YOUR CHILDREN!

Aristotle was the most respected teacher in Athens. The city's best and brightest young men gathered around him at his Lyceum to receive an all-round liberal education, aimed at making them ideal citizens and ideal human beings.

Once, a young mother approached Aristotle. She dreamt of the day when her little son would become Aristotle's student. In her eagerness she wanted the boy to be prepared for it right from his childhood.

"When should I begin training my child, so that he may grow up to be an ideal human being?" she asked the great teacher.

"How old is your child?" enquired Aristotle.

"He is barely five now," said the eager mother.

"Waste no more time, dear lady," said Aristotle, "You are already five years late."

For parents who feel that their children are beginning to lose respect for the ancient Indian values and ideals they cherished, I recommend a 5-point program:

1. Every day, all the members of the family – from the youngest to the eldest – should spend a little time in prayer together. As the saying goes, 'the family that prays together stays together.'

2. Parents must discern that the mother is the greatest influence in the life of a child – especially during the formative years, when the child is in the impressionable, moulding stage. It is under her influence that the child's character is shaped. She can infuse in the children love for their cultural heritage, traditions and values.

3. The father too, has an important role to play. Whatever may be his business preoccupations, he must spend as much time as possible with his children every day.
4. The TV must cease to be the focus of the family in the evenings. The dominant place given to the TV in our homes truly distresses me. In all their free time, the children's eyes are glued to the TV screens. Not only does this harm their eyes, but also makes them sluggish and lethargic. What is worse, the impact of the violence and other undesirable elements shown on the TV makes an indelible negative impression on young minds.
5. Children should be enrolled in weekly classes where they can be introduced to and taught the essentials of India's deathless culture. This is especially important for Indian children who live abroad.

DISCIPLINING YOUR CHILD

How should parents raise their children?

They should raise them by proper precept, guidance, patience and loving discipline.

Without discipline, no art can be learnt – and definitely not the art of living.

Discipline is necessary; discipline is vital. But discipline must not be confounded with suppression or oppression.

There was a little boy, who when asked what his name was, answered, "Haresh Don't."

"Don't?" said the visitor. "That's a strange surname. Are you sure you are Haresh Don't?"

"Sure, I'm sure," said the boy solemnly. "Every time I want to play in the house, mama says, 'Haresh, don't!' Every time I laugh loudly, papa says, 'Haresh, don't!'

This is not the kind of discipline I am talking about. We must treat our children like the intelligent beings that they are.

We must teach them about the values that are essential to them.

We see boys and girls stand up courteously whenever an older person enters the room. Also some children gladly offer their seats to older people on the bus or in a crowded hall. Such courtesy is ingrained in them by the examples set before them by their parents.

Our mothers taught us through precept and example. They narrated to us wonderful stories from the ancient scriptures, took great care to indicate how life might be lived in the right way, by devoting our energies to the service of certain high ideals.

All discipline must be blended with love, so that the child has the assurance that it is for his own benefit, and not in obedience to blind, arbitrary rules.

Many parents don't seem to have the right notion of discipline. Some of them resort to hitting, slapping and pulling the ears. Some resort to constant nagging and verbal abuse.

All this will only frustrate your child and make him defiant.

Discipline is necessary – for children are in the learning stage and their parents are their first and foremost teachers. But love and discipline should go together.

- Give your children your attention when they are well behaved and happy. They must not get the idea that they get noticed only when they are naughty.
- Ensure that rules for good behaviour are mutually accepted by you and your children. Also, let children understand the consequences of breaking rules.

- Always be consistent in applying rules. With older children, especially teenagers, the rules are obviously more stringent.
- It is very important to curb excessive dependence on mobile phones.
- Parents should also be aware of their teenaged children's friends. They must ensure that children do not get into bad company and fall a prey to bad habits.
- It is a good idea to permit your children to bring their friends home once in a while, even if you are too busy to entertain them.
- Excessive pocket money is not at all a good idea!
- Children must be taught that money is to be earned, not merely squandered. Above all do not fall into the trap of offering cash as a reward or incentive for induced behaviour.
- It is a good idea to send children to special yoga or meditation groups with children of their age. These disciplines inculcate will power and spiritual strength.
- Do not pamper your children with needless luxuries. As they grow, they should be encouraged to look after themselves, polish their shoes, clean their rooms and make their beds.
- Temper tantrums and bad behaviour should be ignored, rather than noticed or attended to. Let the anger and violence subside and then make the child understand that such behaviour is not acceptable. But do talk to them and try to understand the cause of their frustration.

A child enjoys revelling in the undivided attention and love that his parents lavish on him.

Transition from a self-centered child to the caring, giving, sharing, less selfish adult, must begin at home. This is why children must be involved in household chores and activities from an early age.

Children should be trained to participate in all routine household activities like cleaning, dusting, wiping, washing, etc.

This will instill in them the spirit of helpfulness and also a sense of respect for manual work. Young boys especially, will learn that it is not their prerogative to be served and waited on.

Children must also be taught to do things as well as they can. Eating at the table with the rest of the family; packing their school bags; playing with their toys and then putting them away – if they are taught the value of perfection in all they do, they will grow up to be neat, tidy, orderly and disciplined in all that they do.

Children should be taught that all work, all tasks constitute worship of God. When things are done to perfection in the spirit of worship, no task will be thought of as too menial or low. Whether you teach them to arrange flowers in a vase or teach them to clean the bathroom, they should do it with the same degree of attention and care.

A HAPPY HOME

It has been said that the home is the door to the Kingdom of God, the kingdom of true happiness. As parents, it is you who can turn a brick-and-mortar house or dwelling into a home where faith and mutual understanding flourish. The mother's role is vital in making the home heaven-like.

Humility and understanding are the keys to harmony and happiness in the home. Parents have to learn to love and appreciate each other and their children, so that familial bonds are strengthened.

Young people should enter into marriage with a serious sense of commitment, integrating head and heart. It is a commitment one makes for a lifetime and not to be taken lightly. When you enter marriage with this sense of commitment, your home is sure to become a temple of love, peace, joy and harmony – a centre of light amidst the encircling darkness. The parents and children from these homes have the wonderful ability to love and serve others and can become the catalysts who transform society.

Parents teach their children to walk and talk. But parents must also learn to understand the child's needs and anxieties and fears and aspirations!

A little boy was holding a sparrow with a broken wing. A kind lady saw him sitting solemnly on the park bench, stroking the wounded bird.

"Sonny, would you like me to take this sparrow home and nurse it back to good health?" she asked him gently.

She assumed that the boy was feeling sorry for the bird, but didn't know what to do with it.

"I promise you I will bring it back here when it is healed," she continued. "Together, we will let it free again."

The little boy thought for a moment. Then he said to her, "Thank you Ma'am. But I would like to take care of the bird myself." He paused, and then added, "You see, I can understand this bird better."

The lady was about to protest, when she saw the boy rise up and walk. He was lame and his leg was in a caliper!

Parents are so used to the idea that they need to care for their children and protect them, that they overlook the fact that even children have minds of their own and need to be allowed to follow their own rainbow, as the saying goes.

Don't thrust your ideas, wishes, hopes and aspirations on your children! If you are a doctor, don't expect your son or daughter to take over your clinic from you. Don't plot out your child's life for him, to the final curve. Respect your child's aspirations and personal preferences. Find out what he likes, what he is good at, and encourage him to excel in what he loves – even if you want something else!

Children are not our possessions to invest as we please.

Comparison and criticism are not conducive to a child's wholesome development. Instead, develop the spirit of understanding and appreciation. Get to know your child's strengths and weaknesses; recognise his limitations; appreciate his talents and unique gifts; encourage him tap into his full potential.

Talk to your child; consult him about his plans for the future. Allow him to grow and evolve in accordance with his own spirit!

Encourage your child to be curious; to ask questions; to indulge in imaginative visions. Don't be hard on creative children who may not always top the class. Above all, don't restrain them, hold them back, or clip their wings.

Dr. Paul Torrance, an authority on IQ, points out that happiness and sound mental health arise out of understanding one's fullest potential.

"Creative people are, in the final analysis, happy people," he says, "provided they are free to create."

Psychologists tell us that today's children are born with much higher IQs than their parents. They are also far more complex beings, born into a world that is becoming more and more complicated.

We need to understand their temperament and adopt our parenting style to their needs, instead of simply treating them as we deem fit.

Temperament has been defined as the innate behaviour style

of an individual, which seems to be biologically determined. Knowing the temperament of your child and treating him with understanding can make all the difference – he will grow up to be a happy, not a troubled child; and you will have the satisfaction of evolving into an understanding, appreciating, accepting parent and not a bitter, frustrated parent!

When you understand a difficult child, you can cope with him better – and you can also help him understand himself. Don't react to his behaviour with anger or frustration – rather, accept his nature and then find a strategy to help him adapt in a way that is socially acceptable.

WALK THE TALK

Children look up to their elders – especially their parents – to set examples before them. It is not enough to talk about virtues and values, but actually demonstrate them.

Even as a child, Sadhu Vaswani was the embodiment of the qualities of compassion, self-sacrifice and humane kindness. While his father, Diwan Lilaram, was a man of learning, faith and *tapasya*, his mother, Varan Devi, was a devotee of the Lord, on whose lips and heart, the Holy Name was constantly present. Brought up under her loving care, it was little wonder that Sadhu Vaswani imbibed her piety and devotion. But even she was surprised by his actions and attitude at times – for he was so different from other children of his age. As he grew up, she saw in him, the qualities of compassion and selflessness. Sometimes, as he sat down to his meals and heard the cry of a passing beggar, he would take his food and share it with the hungry one. Often, his mother would find him awake in the middle of cold, wintry nights.

"What's keeping you awake, my child?" she would enquire solicitously of him. "Are you feeling cold? Shall I wrap one more blanket around you?"

She would be startled by his reply: "Mother, the cold I feel cannot be overcome by a hundred blankets or quilts!"

"I do not understand you, my child!" she would tell him. "Speak to me in plain words, not riddles."

Mark the child's words. He said to her, "Mother, I am thinking of hundreds of homeless ones who, in this severe cold, are lying on the roadside. Their cold seems to pierce my frame." From his early childhood, he was filled with the spirit of compassion for all who were in suffering and pain. He had this sense of identification with the poor and destitute, which marked him distinctly, throughout his life.

This spirit of giving should be inculcated in our children from their earliest days. If we teach them to love others, to care and share, to give to those less fortunate than themselves, we will surely sow the seeds of compassion and selflessness in their receptive hearts, and they will grow to be young men and women of character!

We live in an increasingly competitive world, where the materialistic, acquisitive urge overwhelms all else in us. Selfishness comes easily and naturally to all of us; it is the other, more difficult spirit of selflessness which must be cultivated painstakingly.

Eight-year old Dimple was out with her father on the beach. A balloon vendor came along with beautiful heart-shaped balloons, silver and red in color.

"Papa, papa, can I have a balloon?" begged Dimple. At a little distance from there, a bunch of slum children were watching eagerly – the sight of the balloons was excitement enough for them; there was no question of buying them.

Dimple's father was not a rich man; but the sight of the

eager children and his daughter's pleas worked on his heart. He had kept aside fifty rupees to give Dimple a little treat at one of the food stalls on the beach. On the spur of the moment he gave the fifty rupee note to the balloon vendor and told him to give a balloon each to all the kids standing around. Ten excited kids were laughing and running around and yelling with glee – Dimple, the happiest among the lot. All she wanted was one balloon – her father had given her ten new friends and a whole load of fun!

Let your children grow in the spirit of unselfishness. In ancient times, we are told, no householder would ever sit down to eat with his family, until a poor one had been offered *bhiksha*.

No beggar would be turned away empty handed, from any household!

Translate this beautiful message into deeds of daily life for your children. Teach your children to share and care; to love, give and serve. In this as in all other worthwhile activities, example is always a better teacher than words!

LET NATURE BE THEIR TEACHER

Children must be made to recognise this great truth – that God dwells in every aspect of His creation; and therefore they must be taught to respect and revere all aspects of Nature, including birds, animals, fish and insects; trees and plants and shrubs; even rocks and stones and sand.

Our ancient scriptures tell us that God dwells in all forms and all creatures. In the memorable words of the poet, William Blake:

> To see a world in a grain of sand
> And heaven in a wild flower,
> Hold infinity in the palm of your hand
> And eternity in an hour...

This reflects the belief of the Hindus, the One spirit infuses all Creation – that all that is, is a vesture of the Lord.

Sadhu Vaswani taught us that flowers have their families, even as we do! Therefore, to this day, we avoid plucking flowers for any form of worship or devotion at the Mission campus.

Parents must take the trouble to inculcate in the children love and reverence for nature from an early age. Encourage them to plant seeds and saplings in your garden, balcony or even a window box. Let them watch nature at work, as the seed miraculously sprouts, grows and blooms into flower and leaf.

Teach them to wake at dawn and behold the beauty of the rising sun; teach them to appreciate the myriad hues of twilight and sunset; teach them too, to marvel at the millions of twinkling stars and the silver moon at night.

Nature has a way of influencing our emotions, of instilling calm, peace and serenity into our souls. Children's emotions, especially, can be tuned to respond favourably to the influence of nature.

Books are not the only storehouses of wisdom; sermons are not the only source of moral values; the woods, the trees, the mountains, rivers and valleys can teach our children to revere life and value the great gifts that the Creator has bestowed on us.

If children indulge in cruelty to animals, this will have serious repercussions in their later life. And so, when you see your children being cruel to animals or insects, alarm bells should ring within, to remind you that you are failing in your duty to bring them up as caring, compassionate beings!

Children must be taught that the kindness and compassion they show to all forms of life will do them more good than the creatures for whom they do it!

Nature is also a valuable teacher which teaches us to give and serve – silently!

> God made the sun – it gives
> God made the moon – it gives
> God made the stars – they give
> God made the air – it gives
> God made the clouds – they give
> God made the earth – it gives
> God made the trees – they give
> God made the flowers – they give
> God made the plan – He gives
> God made man – he…?

THE POWER OF PRAYER

To enhance the faith and piety of the children, it is essential that we narrate to them stories of God, and of saints. This will make them aware of the great power, the divine *shakti* that moves the entire universe.

Encourage your children to turn to God in prayer, for all that they need.

I believe that we have two options; either to ask worldly people, or ask God for what we want. Need I say which is the better option?

I believe too, that children should become aware that God is our Father, Mother and Friend.

> *Twameva mata cha pita twameva….*

Why then should we hesitate in asking for anything from God, who is our Father or Mother? To whom else can a child turn, if not to his mother and father?

All God wants is that we turn to Him – for whatever reason.

Let the children pray for whatever they desire – their

consciousness will keep on rising, until one day, they will begin to ask God for his love and his mercy – and nothing else besides!

Teach children too, to realise that God answers all our prayers in three ways:

1) To some of our prayers, He says, "Yes, my child! What you ask is good for you, and I will grant it to you."

2) To some other prayers, He says, "No, my child! What you are asking is not the right thing for you. Therefore, I will not grant it to you."

3) His third answer is: "Wait, my child! I will give you what you want – but in good time. The right time has not yet come."

When prayer becomes a part of your child's life, it lays down the spiritual foundation for his wholesome development. When you teach your child to cultivate absolute faith in God, you are also teaching him to tackle all problems – physical, emotional and spiritual – in the best possible way.

Teach your children too, the value and power of silence. Living in this fast, noisy age, children are often full of restless energy. Teach the children to remember their God and guru first thing, when they awaken, and last thing, before they fall asleep. They should be taught also, to repeat the Name of God during the course of the day. It will give them better concentration and focus and will guard them from all danger and evil.

Teach your children, the secret of joy and peace – make God real in their lives, through the practice of daily prayer!

UNDERSTANDING YOUR TEENAGER

The teen-years, the years of adolescence, the troublesome decade, is actually a period of intense growth – physically, intellectually, emotionally and morally – for the children.

Adolescence can be a difficult and challenging time not only for caring parents – but also for their confused children. Teenagers are often overwhelmed by the physical and emotional changes that they are going through.

In this difficult transition period from childhood to adulthood, they also begin to feel the first stirrings of a strong desire to be independent. This first step towards maturity is in itself positive – but in the teenage years, this impulse is in conflict with the child's obvious dependence on the parents in so many aspects of his life.

The child realises he needs his parents for his sustenance and he does need the security and protection that only their love can give him.

At the same time, he is also trying to assert his own identity, create his own image! Thus many children begin to experiment with clothes, hairstyles and even with new values and a new way of behaviour and speaking. This becomes difficult to handle for the parents and they begin to criticise the children's behaviour, giving them negative feedback and creating bad feelings.

Many children are also uncomfortable about their bodies – especially their overall shape, height and weight. They have lost the happy, unselfconscious attitude of childhood; and they are still years away from the assured self-confidence of young adulthood; trapped in between, they often develop what we call a complex, suffering from low self-esteem.

Teenagers are subject to diverse influences which they are not able to cope with – like peer pressure. Friends and peers tempt them to try cigarettes, alcohol and drugs. In addition, they are also exposed to new conflicting issues such as race, gender, religion and moral values.

One of the most important things that parents need to teach their teenage children is the ability to take responsibility for their own actions and develop a sense of commitment to themselves and their future.

During their teenage, children begin to be more exposed to people and events outside their immediate family circle.

They are making new friends, developing new interests, widening their circle and often have more opportunities to govern their own behaviour – i.e. to behave more or less responsibly, more or less morally, more or less acceptably, more or less in conformity with parental expectations and values.

While they think they are acting independently, they fail to understand that they are rejecting their parents' ideals only to be governed by the influence of their friends.

As parents try to balance precarious demands of career and home, professional and family life, teenage children have to cope with self-governance and independence.

In order to acquire this maturity and independence, they have to develop a sense of autonomy, with a judicial measure of help and support from their parents. My first advice to parents in this connection would be: don't blame it all on your teenager! For example, constant quarrels and heated arguments between the parents, persistent airing of grievances and complaints, and hostility between family members can adversely affect the children's behaviour patterns.

Unable to confront their parents' negative attitude, these children often open up to their friends and teachers, looking for help and support which their parents have failed to give them. But this underlines the fact that the parents have failed the child, let the child down, forcing him/her to look elsewhere for support.

Here are a few things you can do to keep your teenager close to you:

Don't let conversations become conflicts!

Family discussions are good, but needless arguments can cause hostility and resentment in your teenager.

Parents of teenagers should take care not to be harsh and judgemental about their children. Raising your voice, calling names and insulting will not get you very far! Respect your teenager's right to disagree with you; win him over by persuasion, rather than by coercion.

Avoid arguments especially when the situation is volatile and tempers are flaring. It is better to wait till everyone's anger has subsided, and you and your teenager are ready to sit down and sort out your differences. Shouting is not going to be of much help either!

Spend leisure hours with your children!

Plan recreational activities with them – it may be playing board games like Scrabble or Monopoly; it may be going out for a long leisurely walk; or an outing to a park or a museum; or just taking the family out for a drive – such activities help you get close to your teenagers and improves the quality of your relationship with them.

A young Rabbi and his wife were working hard to extend their kitchen so as to make it more modern and comfortable for the family. With three growing children to feed, money was short.

"Papa, Papa, take us out trekking this weekend," begged the eldest son. "Our teacher said the hills are beautiful in the fall, and rare birds come to the mountain springs now."

"Alright," agreed the Rabbi cheerfully. "We shall go trekking this weekend."

Later, as they cleared the kitchen table, the Rabbi's wife said to him, "Why did you have to commit yourself to the kids? We could have put up all the remaining shelves if we had worked through Sunday!"

The Rabbi smiled and said to her, "Honey, twenty, thirty years from now, our children will hardly remember our hard labour to put in the new extension to the kitchen. But believe me, they will remember their trek and the sights they saw and the fun they had! The things that interest us do not always interest our children. We must make it a point to do what they like every now and then. How else can we show them that we really care for them and love them?"

Don't interfere with your teenager's personal tastes, by fussing about minor issues that are really not crucial.

Many parents may not agree with this, but to my mind, such irrelevant issues which you can leave to your children's discretion include the following:

- Their chosen hairstyle
- The setting / decoration of their room
- Their choice of clothes
- Their choice of food and music

There are issues on which parents must have the final word – such as safety in the home and on the road, dating, driving the family car and the amount of pocket money given to children.

Help your teenagers to develop morals and values – not by lecturing to them or enforcing rules on them, but by making them aware of what is right and wrong, and about acceptable and unacceptable behaviour.

This is easier said than done! But you can show them the right way by:

1. Being affectionate, caring parents – but also firm and fair minded at the same time.
2. Laying down rules that are consistent and clear – not confusing and contradictory.
3. Allowing them to take responsibility for decision making and leadership wherever possible.
4. Asking for their help and contribution in family events and community activities.
5. Talking to children about society, politics, religion and spirituality in a way that appeals to them.
6. Encouraging children to express their choices and attitudes to these issues, and trying to understand their reasons for their opinions.
7. Involving the children in constructive community activities such as social service, peace rallies and public discourses by eminent spiritual leaders so that they are exposed to a broader, more selfless view of life.
8. Making them responsible and accountable for their actions, and helping them to grasp the consequences of their own actions, so that they take the corrective measures in a spirit of awareness and understanding.
9. Being good, fair, consistent parents – rather than trying to spoil your child, and doing all you can to win his favour.
10. Practising what you preach. Children learn far more from your life and your behaviour, than from your verbal instructions.

Dealing with Teenagers' Problems

A well-balanced, well-ordered, happy, wholesome family

atmosphere is crucial for the emotional and intellectual development of the children. Experts say that when the home structure is out of balance, meaning, when it is too rigid or too lax – it may result in oppositional or negative behaviour traits. We have to understand that it is extremely difficult to operate as an adult and still crave love and protection as a child. Parents must therefore learn the difficult art of combining love and affection with the ability to soothe the child's anxiety and frustration – even when the child displays negative behaviour patterns.

Look out for warning signals in the teenager's behaviour such as:

- Agitated or restless behaviour and mood swings
- Sudden loss or gain in weight
- Drop in school grades
- Depression, sullenness
- Avoiding the company of family members
- Lack of motivation and enthusiasm
- Lethargy, exhaustion and loss of interest in daily routine
- Rise in inferiority complex and a feeling of worthlessness

These are indications of problems varying from common eating disorders to serious habits like drug abuse.

There are positive attitudes and behaviour patterns that we can put into practice to help protect our children from adverse influences. A home is a door to the Kingdom of God. Creating an atmosphere of love and harmony and peace in every house keeps the family happy and healthy.

FAQs – Parents and Children

Q1.: Can you offer some practical suggestions to parents desirous of bringing up their children in the right way?

Ans.: Here are a few tips which may be found helpful:

1. There is a difference between children and adults. Children live in the now; they are free from anxieties of the past and fear of the future. If a child is in need of something or wants an answer to a question, never say to him, "I shall fulfil your need or answer your question tomorrow or at my leisure."

2. Every child is a human being, with a heart and soul. Never let him feel unwanted. And never forget that the child is an individual, with his own personality and innate talents. Understand him and encourage the creative principle within him to express itself freely. Guide him in a healthy, constructive way by bringing out the best that is in him. Do not impose your will on him and say, "I am a doctor, so my son should become a doctor!"

3. In your treatment towards children, do not discriminate. Do not let them feel that a particular child is your favourite. Children are very sensitive creatures.

4. Keep your child very close to yourself, until he is at least three years of age. He needs your affectionate touch. It is a great blunder to hand over little children to *ayahs* or babysitters.

5. It sometimes becomes very necessary to scold children. Wherever you do so, avoid being emotional. Let your words on such occasions be like whips of love. Explain the fault clearly to the child, and allow him to speak out, if he has anything to say.

6. Even at a young age, children should be trained to attend to household chores. Let them cultivate reverence for manual work.

7. Let children grow in a spirit of unselfishness by training them to share food with the starving ones. Sri Krishna says in the Gita, "He who cooks for himself alone, is a thief!" Before you eat your food, set apart a share for a hungry one – a man, a bird, or an animal. Example is always a better

teacher than precept.

8. The home is a door to the Kingdom of God, the kingdom of true happiness. Let all the members of the family gather together, at a prayer meeting – even if it be for ten to fifteen minutes. This will give a new tone to the home. At a prominent place in your home, keep a big, beautiful picture of some great one – Krishna or Rama, Buddha or Jesus, Zoroaster or Guru Nanak, Mira or Mahavir, Baha'u'llah or Kabir or a saint of humanity – to whom you feel drawn. Whenever you or the children leave the house or enter it, bow down to the picture and offer a small prayer.

Q2.: In families today, parents discipline their children by scolding them and punishing them. They use expressions like, "Bad behaviour, bad girl, bad boy" in the hope of changing their behaviour. Is there an alternative?

Ans.: The alternative is that we must give more time and more attention to our children. And we must give them the pure, selfless love of the heart. We have denied these three things to our children. The truth of the matter is that no child can grow in the right way without love. Today, for the sake of convenience, we have handed the children over to the TV screen. The TV shows them many good things that they should see, but also things they should not see.

Interestingly, it takes longer for the good things to have an effect on the mind of the child, while negative things have a quicker effect on the child. Parents today are busy making money. When I ask them, "Why are you making money?" They answer, "We are making money for our children." But, in the bargain, they lose their children because they don't give them time, attention, or the love of their hearts.

Q3.: Are parents to be blamed for neglecting their children?

Ans.: Not many parents seem to realise their responsibilities towards the children. It was William Tane who said, "Men are generally more careful about the breed of their horses and dogs than their own children."

Of Plato, the great Greek philosopher, it is said that when he found a child doing wrong, he went and corrected the father for it.

Q4.: Dadaji, how could we make the generation gap a pleasant experience?

Ans.: The difficulty with the young people, and I too regard myself as one of them, is that we think that we have mastered the knowledge and wisdom of the whole world. We carry it on the palm of our hands. If only we realise that our parents have passed through many experiences and gathered wisdom from which we can learn, this generation gap will not be a problem. It is because the children feel that their parents don't understand them and do not know anything, that the generation gap is created.

I believe, it is the duty of the parent to become friends with their children when they are in their teens. In their teens, young boys and girls need friends more than parents. The parent must become a friend so that the teenager comes and confides everything in the parents.

Q5.: Dada, why don't parents allow their children to date?

Ans.: Let me answer your question by telling you of a conversation I heard between a girl and her mother.

The girl asked her mother, "Mommy, may I go out this evening with my boyfriend?"

> "No, my child," said the mother.
> "Why, Mommy, don't you trust me?"
> "I do trust you, my child," said the mother.
> "Then, don't you trust my boyfriend?"

"I do trust him," the mother said.

"Then what is the reason?" asked the girl.

And the mother said, "I don't trust the two of you together."

Q6.: How can we accept our parents' views when ours are different? Sometimes we simply cannot agree. What do we do when this happens?

Ans.: There is a great man who observed, "When I was twenty, I felt that my parents were foolish and that I knew everything and they knew nothing. At the age of thirty, I began to see that there was some little wisdom in what my parents said. At the age of forty, I found that there was not a little, but quite a lot of wisdom and common sense in all that they said. At the age of fifty, I have realized that I was a fool to have disregarded what my parents told me."

It is true that there are many points on which youth disagree with adults, especially in this age, which is a transitional period. Values are changing. The values of the older generation are quite different from those of the new generation. One thing, which I feel can help, is to put yourself in the place of your parents. I do not ask you to accept everything that your parents tell you. Maybe your parents do not understand the problems you face. But you must put yourself in their place and consider what your condition would be if your children behaved towards you as you are behaving towards your parents.

Second, the parents should grow in patience. I tell parents, again and again, that they should be friends to their children. They must be easily accessible to the children so that the children will never hesitate to tell them anything. What is happening now is that the children try to hide many things from their parents, which is wrong. This will cut at the very roots of family life.

The attitude of parents and children alike needs to change. Children should be more respectful to their parents. Parents must be more understanding with regard to children's problems. It is only then, that we will be able to build up a happy family life once again. As it is, I am afraid that the gulf between children and parents is widening.

Thirdly, also try to explain to yourself that your parents have passed through their own teenage phase and they have also had to face similar problems. They can give you the right advice. Therefore, listen to them. Think over what they tell you and then do what you consider to be right.

Q7.: How can we develop friendship with our children?

Ans.: To develop friendship with your children you must:

1. Start early. Don't wait until they become teenagers. Then it will be too late.

2. Demonstrate your love to them whenever you can. The first time your children meet you in the morning or when they return from school, greet them warmly. Press their arm; give them a hug or a kiss to assure them that they are important to you.

3. Develop close proximity with your children till they are three years old. At that tender age, they need your affectionate touch and your warm response to everything they do or say.

4. Be a good listener. When the child is talking to you, give him your full attention. Do not dismiss him summarily. Listen to him patiently. Every child wants an interested ear.

5. Try to understand your child. No child expects his parents to agree with him all the time, but he has a right to be understood.

6. Never humiliate your children, especially in the presence of their peers.

7. Try not to let down the trust of a child especially if he trusts

you with a secret, regard it as sacred.

8. Cultivate a rich sense of humour that will help you deal with your children in the right way.
9. Make every meal a time of coming closer to each other. The TV should be switched off.
10. Get to know their friends well, if you want to be friends with their children.
11. Try not to discriminate among children. Let them not have a feeling that one of them is your favourite.
12. Encourage the children to help with domestic chores, especially at an early age. This gives them a sense of belonging, a sense of contribution to the family.
13. Allow the children to dream their dreams! Don't create fantasies about your child's future according to your own expectations and desires. We must not regard our children as an extension of our hopes and dreams.
14. Encourage the children to share food with the starving ones – human beings, birds and animals.
15. Remember, a home is a door to the Kingdom of God. Everyday, at an appointed hour, all the members of the family, young and old, must get together at a prayer meeting. This will create a new atmosphere of love and harmony and peace in every house. The family that prays together, stays together!

KARMA

IS GOD FAIR?

Our life on this earth is full of pleasant and unpleasant experiences. We pass through difficult times as well as enjoyable times. And even as we move along the pathways of life a period comes – a time comes in the life of each one of us, when we are confronted by the question: Is God Fair?

There are times when we are happy; we laugh and sing; we are content with the way things are; everything seems to be going our way; we have all that we need, and many of the things we want. We say, God is gracious; God is great; God is generous! But a stage comes when we hit a rough patch; we pass through a trying phase; we encounter not just one or two, but a series of bitter experiences. Nothing seems to go right with us. We are confronted by problems and sufferings whichever way we turn. It is then that out of the very depths of our hearts comes this cry: Is God Fair? Is He just?

There was a sister whom I met. She had been married to a kind and loving man. Soon after their marriage, they went on a honeymoon. They were away for a fortnight – which she found to be the most beautiful period of her life. Her husband loved her dearly; he was a wonderful man in every which way. The honeymoon was indeed like a wonderful dream!

But all dreams come to an end – and as the happy couple were returning home, their car was involved in a terrible accident. A truck collided head-on with the vehicle, and the young husband was killed on the spot.

"It's true God gave me a wonderful husband," the woman told me. "But what's the point of snatching him away from me, barely two weeks after we were married? If he had to die so soon, why did God let me get married at all? Is God fair? Is God really fair?"

WHY ME?

Our sages have repeatedly emphasised one fact: every incident, every accident that happens to us, happens because we deserve it. Good and bad fortune are not handed to us on a platter; we have earned them through our own actions. Every action we perform, every incident that befalls us, is a reaction to our past actions. But when misfortune strikes, we fail to apprehend this.

A woman who devoted the best years of her life to social service, was pleasant and affable, obliging by nature, and brought joy and comfort into the lives of those that were in need. She never ever thought of her own comfort and convenience, but went out of her way to serve as many as she could with her kindness and love.

One day, as she was walking along briskly, she suddenly lost her balance and slipped; but she picked herself up and carried on, heedless of the pain. A few days later, as she was returning home at night, she stumbled and fell across the threshold.

She was worried, and went to her doctor for a check-up. The doctor examined her thoroughly and diagnosed her condition to be multiple sclerosis. She had never even heard of the term before. "What is multiple sclerosis?" she asked in perplexity.

The doctor explained to her that multiple sclerosis is a degenerative nerve disease which gathers momentum with the passage of time. It would affect her mobility in due course. She could be confined to a wheelchair. The doctor also added that the time may come when she could lose all bowel and bladder control. She would be dependent on others for all her routine chores.

The woman was dumbfounded. "Why me?" was her first reaction. Why did this happen to me of all the people? When all my friends are living very healthy and very happy lives, why did this have to happen to me? Is God Fair?

When they are faced with unpleasant or negative experiences, people react stereotypically: Why me? Why did it have to be like this? These are the cries we hear at such times. The attitude of the sufferers is that they are victims – innocent victims – while someone else is the culprit, responsible for inflicting them with undeserved pain.

While we can sympathise with this attitude, we must realise that this will deprive us of the opportunity to reflect, introspect, and thus recognise our own responsibility for our actions. In fact, by blaming others for our ills, we are only worsening the situation, or giving rise to new problems.

When we face whatever happens to us in a spirit of acceptance, we ward off many negative feelings such as hatred, envy, malice and resentment. We rise above a sense of personal injustice and grow in the secure sense of divine universal justice. In such a spirit and such a mood, despair and misery are kept out, and we are not overwhelmed by what happens to us.

A few years ago, I was told about this girl, who was a brilliant student at a University. She was doing her M.B.A. and she was expected to top her class. She was sure to get placed as a well-paid executive in one of the best companies in her city. Her mind was totally set on a professional career, and she was not interested in marriage at all.

Her parents were very anxious to get her married. They had come across a handsome, wealthy young man who had flown in from the U.S. to visit his family. They were convinced that he would make an excellent husband to their brilliant daughter. They cajoled her into marriage with this young man.

They were married shortly, went on a short honeymoon, and everything seemed perfect. Soon afterwards, the husband had to leave for the U.S. The girl had to wait for six months, until her visa formalities were completed. When everything was settled, she flew to the U.S. to join her husband.

He was not there at the airport to receive her when she arrived. Just imagine the plight of a young girl who is flying into a foreign country for the first time in her life – there was no one to meet her. With the help of a kind-hearted fellow traveller, she managed to reach her husband's house. Sure enough, he opened the door. But it was not the happy ending to her story.

"Look here," he said to her harshly. "I don't want you here with me. I am married to an American girl, and you can't stay here with us."

The girl was thunderstruck. Why did he have to spoil her life and ruin her career and her future? Why did this have to happen to her – she didn't even want to get married in the first place!

You could not blame that girl if she raised the question: Is God fair? Why me?

WHEN BAD THINGS HAPPEN TO GOOD PEOPLE

I know a young woman who lives in Singapore. She is pious and God-fearing, and an active member of a yoga club in Singapore. A few years ago, she travelled to India along with her family members. They visited a number of sacred shrines. They met holy men, spiritual teachers whom they respected, and sought their blessings. Their trip to this country was veritably a pilgrimage. They returned to Singapore, spiritually rejuvenated.

A few days thereafter, their office premises were gutted by fire, and precious documents and equipment were destroyed. The girl was distraught. Why did this have to happen to us, she cried. We visited India in a spirit of reverence; we sought the blessings of so many holy ones! How could God do this to us? Is God fair? Is He really fair?

The story is the same wherever I go. People say to me: we have been honest and hardworking; we have not hurt or exploited anyone; we have done as much good as we could – and yet we have had to suffer.

Some people believe that there are certain disciplines, certain practices which they must carry out – certain obligations they owe to God; and if they fail to fulfil them, they or their dear ones will be punished. One such woman met me when I visited Ottawa in Canada. She told me that she recited the second, twelfth and the eighteenth chapters of the Gita every day, before she took her lunch. She also observed the *Satyanarayan* fast every month. But during a whole month, she missed out on the recitation and the fast, due to one reason or the other. The day after the missed *Satyanarayan* fast, her husband, who was perfectly healthy and normal, suffered a stroke, and had remained paralysed since then. The woman put to me the question that was uppermost in her mind: Has this anything to do with my failure to read from the scriptures and observe the fast? Is there any cause-and-effect relationship between the two? Is God such a rigid taskmaster? Is He really fair?

A learned Rabbi has written a book entitled *When Bad Things Happen to Good People*. In this book he tells us how suddenly, his three-year-old son was afflicted with a disease called progeria. Neither he nor his wife were even aware of a disease of that name. What is progeria, they asked the doctor, bewildered by the suddenness of it all.

The effect of the disease, the doctor explained, would be that the boy would not grow taller than three feet; that he would remain bald, and would age rapidly. Even as a child, he would have the appearance of an old man.

The Rabbi was grief stricken. Why has God permitted an innocent child to become the victim of such a terrible disease? This little boy has never harmed or hurt anyone. Why is he being exposed to such physical and psychological torture?

In his book, the Rabbi gives us several other cases similar to this one, and comes to a startling conclusion:

> God is not omnipotent, all-powerful, as we believe Him to be. God has limited power. Within these limitations, God can exercise His discretion. But there are certain grey areas where He is helpless. There are certain forces that He cannot control. And when these forces operate, God has no way of helping you. His power is limited and defined.

This is the conclusion that the learned Rabbi reaches in his book. "Here was I, who had dedicated my entire life to the service of God," the Rabbi tells us. Why did such a terrible affliction strike my child? Thus, he concludes, there are several incidents and accidents of life over which God has no control. When such troubles and trials confront man, God remains a passive spectator, who is powerless to intervene.

And so we return to the question which has haunted us again and again – Is God Fair?

GOD IS FAIR

If you look upon life as a journey, as many great writers have done, then you will know that this journey takes us at times through pleasant green meadows and lush river valleys; but at other times, this journey takes us through dry, arid deserts and dark, mysterious woods. When times are good, we are happy, we rejoice and offer gratitude to the Lord. But when things go wrong, we lose our equilibrium. We begin to question the justice of the universe. It is at such moments that this question arises in the heart within – Is God Fair? Is God Really Fair?

Before you finally decide whether God is fair or otherwise, I would wish to draw your attention to four very important points:

1. We have all been given the freedom of choice. Man is free to choose – between vice and virtue, good and evil, selfishness and service. Man can choose to be selfish or unselfish. He can choose to be a sinner or a saint. The choice is entirely his.

   But remember, if the right to freedom of choice is vested within him, it follows that the responsibility for his actions also rests with him; for we cannot have rights without responsibilities. At every step on the road of life, we have the freedom to choose the direction in which we move.

   The path of good, leads me forward; I progress; I evolve spiritually. Following the path of evil, I regress; I am pushed backwards. If I choose wrong over right, evil over good, how can I blame God for what results from my action?

   This is the difference between men and animals. Animals do not have a mind or will of their own, to act consciously by a considered choice. They act without ulterior motive. They are only impelled by their instincts. Suppose a man is crossing a jungle; he is confronted by a hungry man-eater who leaps on him, attacks him, tears his flesh to pieces and feeds on him! How can any blame accrue to the animal in this terrible incident? The animal was hungry; it killed and ate its victim. It was only acting according to its instincts, for it can act in no other way. Whereas, if you or I were hungry, we do have a choice. We can lay our hand on the nearest chicken or lamb that we find, kill the dumb, defenseless animal, and feed on its flesh. Or we can shun this kind of violence, and choose the food of *ahimsa,* in the form of fruits and vegetables. The choice is ours, and the responsibility for our action rests with us. If we make the wrong choice, we must prepare to face up to its unpleasant consequences.

When we make the choice between good and evil, right and wrong, we determine the consequences of our own action. Amidst joy and pleasure and success, we invariably forget God; but the moment sorrow strikes, we rush to God with prayers and entreaties. We complain, "What have you done? Why is this happening to me?" If I have chosen the wrong/evil path, and I have encountered a bitter experience which I cannot swallow, how can I question God's justice? Is it fair on my part to ask, "Is God Fair?" Is it fair to blame God for the choices that I have made?

2. There are numerous occasions in life when people get things that they never expected, or things that they have longed for all their life. After a long and frustrating wait, childless couples are blessed with an offspring. Someone in dire need of money hits a jackpot. Another gets a long-awaited promotion. None of them ever think of telling God, "Why have you done this to me?" They simply assume that they have every right to the happiness that has come their way; they take it all for granted.

3. God's tender mercy to us is boundless – if only we took the trouble to fathom the extent of His kindness. To people who come to me with bitter complaints against life, I pass on two sheets of paper. On one sheet I ask them to write all the cruel, the unfair, the unjust, the tyrannical, the dishonest and crooked things that they have done. On the other one, I ask them to write down all the good, the noble, the unselfish

deeds that they have done in their lifetime. This is an exercise I recommend to you also, for it can be a real eye-opener for you. When you have prepared these two lists, you will find that one list is much longer than the other.

This is the case with most people – where their bad actions will by far outweigh the few good deeds they may have done. With such certain knowledge of our own balance sheet of right and wrong, how can anyone of us claim that God has been unfair or unjust to us?

4. The last and the most important thing we must note is that when we suffer, God always gives us the strength and wisdom to bear the suffering. For these are just two sides of the same coin – sorrow and wisdom, suffering and endurance. Look at the coin – on one side is suffering; on the other side is the wisdom and the strength to bear that suffering. Never, ever does God send suffering to us, unaccompanied by the strength and wisdom to cope with it. That is why we continue to live, that is how mankind has survived personal and public calamities, and still continues to survive and flourish. The very fact that we are all alive and breathing, is a testimony to this great truth – that we invariably conquer suffering with God-given strength and wisdom.

It is undeniably true, that with every suffering comes the healing mercy of God. With suffering comes wisdom and strength.

To summarise, when you consider these points –

- The freedom of choice that we enjoy
- The compensations and rewards that life offers to us
- God's tender mercy to us
- The wisdom and the strength He sends to us along with suffering

Is it fair then to question God's justice? Is it fair to ask – Is God Fair?

THE LAW OF KARMA

When Dr. Annie Besant, the founder of the famous Theosophical Society of India, was a young woman, she worked on the editorial staff of a prestigious magazine called *The New Review*. She was an intellectual woman, given to mature reflection and logical thinking. She gave birth to a baby who fell seriously ill soon after birth. The baby was running high fever, and as the temperature rose, the infant developed convulsions. Annie Besant was distraught at the sight of her little child going through these violent fits. She could not bear to think of her innocent baby being put through such suffering.

She virtually gave up all faith and belief in God after this happened. She became an agnostic. She spoke to preachers and religious teachers. No one could answer her questions satisfactorily: "Where is God's love and compassion? Why is this child, who hasn't even hurt a fly, subject to such suffering?" They do not have an answer to such questions in Western philosophy, and Annie Besant got no answers.

She came across a book by Mme. H. P. Blavatsky, entitled *The Secret Doctrine*. The editor had sent it to her for the purpose of review. As Annie Besant began to read the book, a new understanding dawned on her, and she was deeply impressed by its contents. One of the chapters in the book was entitled, "Karma and Reincarnation". She read it again and again – and began to see life in a new perspective. She seemed to have found, at last, answers to the questions she had been asking.

She understood that the present life was not the first life, the only life lived by her, or her child. She had lived many, many, other lives before she had entered this body – likewise, her infant. It was due to the child's actions in those earlier births, that it was going through certain consequences in this birth. The infant had done something earlier, the effect of which, the fruit of which it was now faced with. The whole thing was crystal clear; the mystery was unravelled. She began to understand things, which were inexplicable earlier.

Once we understand this doctrine, the answer to the vexing question, "Is God Fair?" becomes very clear.

So we come to the question: what exactly is this doctrine? What is karma?

The law of karma may be described as the law of causation – the foundation on which this universe evolves. It affects all aspects of our existence – spiritual, psychic, physical; it influences our thoughts, intentions, motives and actions. It embraces our past, present and future, linked in a continuous cause-effect relation. The impact of this law is inescapable and inexorable. Its effect, reaction and response are absolutely impartial. We could say that it is the law of karma that upholds *dharma*, and maintains justice, equity, order and balance in the universe. The law of karma operates on individuals, as well as groups, communities, races and nations.

Any action, thought or feeling generated by an individual, brings with it certain indelible impressions, which are stored in the mind as *samskaras*. Every act, thought or feeling leaves behind a trace, which has the power to bring joy or sorrow. These traces, or *karmic* residue, can bring about consequences on three different levels:

1. The type of next birth – bird, animal, plant or human
2. Life span – long-lived or short-lived
3. Life experiences – pleasurable or painful

THE SCHOOL OF LIFE

To return to the question we raised earlier: is God unfair and unjust? The answer is that there is no question of any injustice in God's dispensation.

Each one of us has been given a field of life. We are free to sow whatever we want in this field, which is our *karmakshetra*. Only one condition binds us; we must reap what we sow. We must eat the fruits of our own harvest. Every thought I think, every word I utter, every deed I perform, every emotion, every feeling, every wish that awakens within me – these are all seeds that I am sowing in the field of my life. In course of time, these seeds will germinate and bear fruit. Bitter or sweet they may be – but I shall have to eat those fruits. No one else can eat them for me. Where then is the question of God being unfair or unjust to me?

The trouble is that man in his ignorance, commits errors and misdeeds. His wrong acts add up to his karma. His karma binds him to its consequences. What we must seek, therefore, is liberation from the bonds of karma.

Life is like a school for human souls. We have all come to this school to learn valuable lessons, to reach certain conclusions, to attain certain goals, that we may obtain knowledge of the truth that is worth knowing.

The Gita tells us that the body is merely a garment worn by the soul during its earthly existence. The body is born and it dies.

The soul is deathless, eternal; fires cannot burn it, weapons cannot cleave it; air cannot dry it; waters cannot drown it. We are born and reborn upon this earth, so that we may grow in perfection and ultimately achieve liberation – our true state. We are all students in the school of life; experience is our teacher, and it offers us valuable lessons that we may evolve spiritually, and attain the liberation that we seek.

We pass through varied experiences here; for the lessons that I have to learn are vastly different from the lessons you will have to learn. The law of karma is not punitive; it does not wreak vengeance, and it is the fine art by which we may eventually transcend the cycle of birth and death. God's Law of Karma works to put us on the path to perfection.

God loves us deeply, and therefore, through the operation of the law of karma, he places us in such an environment where we may recognise our *atma shakti* (spiritual strength) and awaken to the true knowledge of the Self. In our ignorance and immaturity, we may regard this as a form of punishment; but like the kind and caring teacher, God knows that these experiences are vital to our spiritual growth.

THE LAW OF THE BOOMERANG

Everything that happens to man is of his own doing. In other words, man is the builder of his own destiny. Destiny is not something that has been imposed on him from without. He is the architect of his own future. God has given man complete freedom of choice. We can choose between good and evil.

Sadhu Vaswani described the principle of karma as the principle of a boomerang. What you send, comes back to you! Do you gossip about another? You will be gossiped about.

Do you send out loving thoughts to others? Do you pray for struggling souls? Do you serve those who are in need? Are you kind to passers-by, the pilgrims on the way who seek your hospitality? Then remember, sure as the sun rises in the East, all these things will return to you, making your life beautiful and bright as a rose garden in the season of spring!

The law of karma is thus the law of the boomerang. It is an inviolable law that governs the universe from end to end.

THE GOOD THAT YOU DO

The subtle effect of an action (karma) is to reflect the action back to you. The law of karma states that you are repaid by the same pleasure or pain that you bestow on others through your action.

There was a woman who always baked an extra *chapati*, when she prepared the meals for her family. She kept the extra *chapati* on the window-sill for whoever would take it away. Every day, a hunchback came and took away the *chapati*. Instead of expressing gratitude, he muttered the following words before he went his way:

> The evil you do remains with you:
> The good you do comes back to you!

This went on, day after day. Every day, the hunchback came, lifted the *chapati*, and uttered the same words.

Every day, as the woman placed the *chapati* on the window-sill she offered a prayer for her son who had gone abroad to seek his fortune. For many months she had had no news of him. She prayed for the safe return of her son.

Though she left the extra chapati as an offering to God, she was irritated by what she thought to be sheer ingratitude on the part of the beggar. One day, her annoyance turned to destructive hatred. "I shall get rid of this hunchback," she said to herself. She added poison to the *chapati* she prepared for him! As she was about to keep it on the window-sill, her hands trembled. "What is this that I am doing?" she said to herself. Immediately, she threw the *chapati* into the fire, prepared another and kept it on the window-sill. As usual the hunchback came, picked up the *chapati* and muttered the words:

> The evil you do remains with you:
> The good you do comes back to you!

The hunchback proceeded on his way, blissfully unaware of the war raging in the mind of the woman.

That evening, there was a knock on the door. As she opened it, she was surprised to find her son standing in the doorway. He had grown thin and lean. His garments were tattered and torn. He was hungry, starved and weak. Looking at his mother, he said: "Mother, it's a miracle that I have been able to reach you. When I was but a mile away, I was so famished that I collapsed. Just then, an old hunchback passed by. I begged of him for a morsel of food, and he was kind enough to give me a whole *chapati*. As he gave it to me, he said, 'This is what I eat every day. Today, I shall give it to you, for your need is greater than mine!'"

As the mother heard those words she turned pale. She leaned against the door for support. She remembered the poisoned *chapati* she had made that morning. Had she not hearkened to the voice of her conscience and burnt it in the fire, that *chapati* would have cost her, her son's life. It was then that she understood the meaning of the hunchback's words:

The evil you do remains with you:
The good you do comes back to you!

When you do good, remember that good will return to you. The evil you do remains with you!

FATE AND FREE WILL

Is man a free agent? Or is he a puppet in the hands of destiny? Can he change his own fate?

Let me quote a saying I hear very often:

Bani banayi ban rahi, aab kuch banani nah...

There are some people who will tell you everything is already 'written', that you cannot change what is to happen. Whatever you do, whatever efforts you put in, you will not be able to change your destiny.

But then, as we saw earlier, we came to the conclusion that man is endowed with a free will, man has the freedom to change his destiny at every step, in every round of life.

The two different answers given to our question are the two sides of the same coin. The first is that man is a prisoner of his own fate. No matter how valiant his efforts, he cannot change the contours of his destiny.

The second answer is that man is absolutely free. He has the freedom of choice to act – to choose right or wrong. At every step of life, he can make the effort to improve his condition. Through his actions, he can actually succeed in changing his own karma and thus altering his own destiny.

The first karma is *ichcha shakti* – the freedom of choice; the second is *prarabdha* karma – our accumulated karma. Only when the two go together, can we act in any sense of the term. They are like the twin blades of scissors. When the two blades act together, the scissors does its job. You cannot cut a piece of cloth with just one blade of a pair of scissors. Likewise, fate and free will are both necessary for action. Karma determines the type of family into which you are born, your religion, your race and the type of body in which you are born. These are things you cannot change.

There was a man who spent a fortune, trying to increase his height by a couple of inches. He could not achieve this; his height could not be increased even by one millimeter. But there is a place for free will even in such cases. Whatever be your fate, you always have this choice – of reacting to your fate in a positive or negative manner. This is always within your power!

RESCRIPTING YOUR DESTINY

The concept of preordination holds that God settles and fixes the destiny of a man even before he is born into the world. This is neither logical, nor tenable. It makes man a puppet, a thing of straw, and, what is worse, it makes God partial, whimsical, unfair and unjust. Man's freedom of choice, his sense of moral responsibility and his independence are all nullified. Why should God make some of us rich, powerful and successful, while some of us are condemned to poverty, illness and despair?

Questions like these – and many more – will remain unanswered if we accept the theory of pre-ordination. On the other hand, the Doctrine of Karma is lucid and clear: everyone reaps the fruits of his or her own actions. It is thus essentially one of hope and encouragement. It is the best motivation we can have for right thinking, right action and right living. If only we understood this law in its fullness, our lives would be beautiful indeed! We would learn the virtues of peace and contentment. We would bear the burdens of life with patience and acceptance, and we would rejoice even in suffering.

Each one of us is a child of God and He wants us to be happy, healthy, prosperous, successful, and to enjoy all the good things He has created. We deny ourselves these bounties, only because of our karma. Change your karma and you will change the conditions in which you live!

MORE ABOUT KARMA

Some scholars compare karma to energy. We create energy through our thoughts, words and deeds – and in time, this energy comes back to us, maybe through other people. Karma has also been compared to the law of gravity, for it acts equally upon us all. The law of karma is dynamic and positive; it is not passive or defeatist.

Many people equate karma with evil, sin – with whatever is bad. This is probably because we become aware of karma only when we face difficult situations. Karma is equated even with fate or destiny – a preordained destiny over which we have no control.

Someone utters kind words to you – and you feel peaceful, happy and relaxed. Another person utters harsh, unkind words – and you are disturbed and upset. The kindness and harshness will return to the people who caused them – maybe, at a later time.

Karma is thus, a natural law of the mind. We generate our own karma with our thoughts, words and deeds. It would be quite true to say that our thoughts create our karma – good, bad or indifferent!

INTIMATIONS OF IMMORTALITY

Many philosophers believe, that when we are born into this world, we still carry with us beautiful visions of Heaven which is our true home, as well as memories of our past births which are deeply embedded in our soul. In this state of grace, our souls are radiant, and we are invested with a boundless capacity to give and receive love, to radiate joy and peace, and to experience true bliss.

We have seen babies smile beautifully in their sleep, also, the faraway look in their eyes, as they seem to see through us into eternity. This is a sign that as infants, we carry with us visions of immortality.

Babies are in a state of joy and grace. They are like the lilies of the field: they toil not, nor do they fear. They do not worry about the past or the future. They are secure in the present moment.

Alas, the spotless state of our soul is soon clouded by the indoctrinations of the world. Sad to say, even our parents, teachers, elders, the society we live in, inculcate wrong, false values in us. We are taught to love money, power, pleasure – all the shadow shapes of this world of *maya* (illusion).

Once, a mother saw her three-year-old son, bending low over the cradle of his newborn baby brother. She went closer to investigate what the boy was up to. She heard him whisper in the baby's ears, "You must tell me about God and Heaven. I'm afraid I'm beginning to forget it all!"

We have so much to learn from our children, before they forget it all. We have been children, in this life and in the many lives before this one. We too have forgotten! If we wish to attain liberation, we must remember! We must renounce the worldly indoctrination that only leads to grief, despair and misery! We must reclaim our capacity for joy and love!

Dr. Brian Weiss, a distinguished psychiatrist, tells us that he heard this incident from a young mother. The family's pet dog had just died, and she had come out of the room to make a phone call to the vet, to make arrangements for the interment of the dog's body.

When she returned to the room, she was startled to see that her two year-old son had wrapped up the dog from head to tail – with band-aid and butter! "Why….. why have you done this?" she stammered.

"Mommy, I'm just making sure he slides into heaven, smooth and fast," was the toddler's reply.

When she mentioned the incident to a friend, she was told that this was, in fact, the burial practice of ancient Egyptians. She was even shown a book, with the picture of a buried dog, which looked exactly like their dog! She concluded that her son had been an Egyptian in his previous birth.

As we grow, we forget all our past experiences from previous lives.

KARMA IS AN OPPORTUNITY

A Western thinker writes:

We have debts that must be paid. If we have not paid out these debts, then we must take them into another life… you progress only by paying your debts…

Debts that must be paid – that sums up the concept of karma. But I would add that karma is not just a burden that you have to carry. It is also an opportunity to learn, a chance to practise love and forgiveness, a chance to learn lessons that are valuable to us. Karma offers us the chance to wipe our dirty slate clean, to erase the wrongdoings of the past.

Karma is a uniquely Hindu concept. But its basic tenets are reflected in many religions. Thus, the Bible tells us, "As you sow, so shall you reap." And further, "God will render to every man according to his deeds." Judaism teaches, "He who is liberal will be enriched, he who waters will himself be watered."

I always say that people who hurt and kill in the name of religion, are killing their own brethren, for the surest way to reincarnate in a particular race or religion, is to hate that particular religion. It has truly been said that religious hatred and intolerance will become like the express train that will carry you into the religion you hate!

Karma is an opportunity to learn; karma is an opportunity to evolve spiritually; karma is an opportunity to repay all outstanding debts, so that we may be free to move onward, Godward!

HOW TO CREATE GOOD KARMA

We must learn to cultivate the ability to master the working of karma in our daily lives, so that we create our own good karma. Here are a few principles that may help you in this regard.

Forgive and forget

Revenge and retaliation are best left to time. Let us, in the words of the Lord's prayer, "forgive those who trespass against us." The impulse to take revenge only leads to negative karma. As Mahatma Gandhi observed, "The law of an eye for an eye makes the whole world blind."

Learn to be responsible for your thoughts, words and actions

We must accept the responsibility for all that happens to us. We always practise this perfectly, when good things happen to us. If I stand first in an examination, I am happy to take all the credit. If my business prospers, I attribute it to my hard work and sagacity. But what if I am faced with troubles and difficulties? What, when the going is rough?

We only accumulate negative karma if we continue to blame others for our failures and troubles. Instead, we must learn to accept the responsibility for our own destiny, and sow the seeds of good karma.

Refrain from causing pain to others

When we harm others, we are paving the way for harming ourselves in the future! We will do well to pause before we act in anger, and reflect upon the consequences of our action.

Seek guidance from your guru, or a spiritual elder

Most of us lack the mental and spiritual strength to wage the battle of life alone. But the wonderful thing is we are not alone! Divine guidance for divine grace is always available to those who seek it. Turn to your guru or to a spiritual teacher who will help you overcome negative karmic patterns.

Do all that you can to mitigate the effect of past karma

Not only must we accumulate good karma for the future, we must also rid ourselves of the effect of past karma.

While it is true that we carry upon us the burden of our past karma, the negative effects of the burden can be mitigated to a large extent by our good deeds in this life.

Work towards your own liberation

Many of us are apt to imagine that liberation from the bonds of karma, freedom from the cycle of birth and death, is not attainable for the likes of us. When we set our sights firmly on the goal, we accelerate the pace of our own spiritual evolution. This is achieved through *bhakti* (devotion), *seva* (service) and *sadhana* (practise of austerities like meditation).

By consciously setting out to purify ourselves thus, we can accelerate the process of our own karma and get closer to *mukti* (liberation).

THE TWO SELVES WITHIN YOU

There are two 'selves' within us, the higher and the lower. The higher nature impels us to overcome all that is negative in us – greed, envy, anger and hatred – but the lower nature is inclined to suppress all that is positive, and leads us towards evil. The human soul is torn between these two conflicting forces of good and evil. It is only when we strengthen the positive forces within us, and identify with our Higher self, that we can attain God-realisation.

When scientists succeeded in splitting the atom, they rejoiced that they had discovered the means to create abundant energy and power; but what happened thereafter was something horrible. This secret of splitting the atom was misused and abused, to rain death and destruction on Hiroshima and Nagasaki.

We know that science and technology can be used for good or bad purposes. It is only when we use it wisely and well that it can truly be a blessing to humanity.

So it is with our lives. It is only when we will live consciously, vigilantly, aware of everything we say and do, that we can achieve good karma. We need to act with wisdom, enlightenment and balance.

Karmic actions lead to results that may affect us in this birth, or in lives to come. Thus, karma is closely linked with the concept of rebirth.

This leads us to the next question. What happens to us in the interim between death and rebirth? Are all souls condemned to be born again and again – caught in the cycle of birth, death and rebirth?

According to *Vedanta* wisdom, there are four possibilities open to the soul after death:

1. For one who has attained enlightenment during this life, there is total liberation from the cycle of birth and death. Such a one attains *sadyah mukti* or instantaneous liberation and is not born again.

2. For one who has not attained liberation, but achieved purity of mind and devotion to Brahman, there is a force which pushes the soul beyond the pull of this world and towards liberation. This is *krama mukti* – gradual or sequential liberation. In this process, the soul is led along a path of light and so attains an increasing expansion in consciousness until liberation is attained.

3. For one who has tried to live a virtuous life, but is not ready for liberation, there is a finite period of existence on the astral plane, where the astral body experiences pleasurable conditions. This is known as *swarga*. It is not liberation, but a relative experience of pleasure. This finite period is brought to an end when the soul's good karma is exhausted, and the soul is reborn into a new life.

4. For one who has accumulated no good karma at all, there is the painful fourth alternative – a period of intense suffering for the sake of expiation or purification. But this period also comes to a close when the sinful karma is exhausted, and the soul is reborn in a new embodiment.

Thus, in the first two cases, liberation is attained. In the third and the fourth, the soul must return to earth for the sake of its further evolution – after a period of either heavenly pleasure or hellish suffering. In these cases, karma will determine its next embodiment. For there are residues, remnants of karma that are not exhausted in the life-after-death state, be it heaven or hell. It is this residue or remnant that influences one's rebirth and life experiences. In other words, none of us is born into this world with what is called a clean-slate. Even what we consider to be hereditary traits are in reality determined by the karma of previous lives.

TYPES OF KARMA

Karma, as we have read and understood, is a universal law. Every thought or impulse is a seed we sow in the subconscious mind; this impulse forms an impression; this impression is nurtured and grows into an act. Every act we perform has an effect on our life.

All actions performed in the true spirit of *dharma* or righteousness contribute to the peace, harmony, balance and integrity of our lives. All action pertaining to *adharma* produces disorder, disharmony and strife. Thus is cosmic justice rendered, and the scales of the universe held even.

In order to understand this balance of cosmic justice, it is necessary for us to grasp three different aspects – three different types of karma:

1. ***Kriyaman* or *agami karma:*** *Kriyaman karma* is that which cancels itself there and then. You take a bath; it is an action by which your body is cleansed; this is the effect which is immediately achieved. Causes subside, when the effect is produced. Action comes to an end, when the reaction sets in. Thus, *kriyaman karma* is not carried forward. Any action of yours that leads to immediate result is *kriyaman karma*. Action and reaction – *kriya and pratikriya* are both completed;

they have no effect on your future actions.

2. **Sanchita karma**: *Sanchita karma* is the sum total and store of all our actions, good and bad in the sequence of innumerable lives that we have lived. All of this is recorded and preserved.

   All this karma does not fructify, does not bear fruit at once. Only a small part of it fructifies in any one birth or embodiment. The rest of it remains accumulated – awaiting its fructification.

   Our *sanchita karma* keeps on growing; in fact, it grows from birth to birth; it has been accumulating on a spiritual record through innumerable lives from time immemorial. The load of *sanchita karma* that each one of us carries is tremendous – a heavy load indeed. *Sanchita karma* is karma that waits for an opportunity. It emphasises the law that you cannot get away with anything. Neither did King Dashratha get away nor King Dhritrashtra. We have to pay our debts, we must reap what we have sown – if not in this birth, in subsequent births!

3. **Prarabdha karma**: This third type of karma is that part of our karma which matures, comes to fruition in one particular birth.

   Those of us who have been given this gift of human birth, we may be sure that it is the result of very good karma. Thus *prarabdha karma* on which our present existence is based, is often referred to as fate, destiny or luck, in common parlance.

   Prarabdha karma is a part, or a fragment of *sanchita karma* which has fructified in this birth. It is *prarabdha karma* which determines the family into which you are born. It determines the race, the nation in which you take birth; it also determines your sex, the type of body you will acquire, etc. Remember this – your wealth is predetermined. You may keep working all day, all night to get more money – but only that much money will come to you, which is permitted by *prarabdha*. Even if you get more, you will lose it through speculation, theft, etc. It is only when this *prarabdha karma* is exhausted that your physical body will drop down, and you will get a period of freedom, until you wear another physical body – to work out more karma that may have fructified in the meanwhile. Our present life – our condition, our circumstances, even our longevity, are all determined by *prarabdha karma*.

In total contrast to this, we also come across tragic deaths of the very young, including babies, small children and newly married couples. We are shocked, horrified by such untimely deaths. The answer is simple. Their fructified karma has been exhausted. The purpose for which they had to assume their physical body in this lifetime has been completed. Back their souls must return, to reap the rewards of this lifetime.

Not a day more or less, not a second more or less can we live upon this earth, than the duration of life that has been ordained to us by our own *prarabdha karma*. When we understand this, we will not be baffled by 'untimely' deaths or prolonged lives. Each soul must live out its allotted term upon this earth, until its fructifying karma lasts – until the fruit has been eaten, to the last sweet or bitter portion.

However, there are a few important observations which I must make at this stage, with regard to the three types of karma that we have been discussing.

In any particular birth, while I am exhausting my *prarabdha karma*, the karma that has fructified, I am simultaneously creating new karma. I may exhaust in this birth, one hundred thousand *prarabdha* karmas, but in the process, I create millions of other karmas, and these are added to my store of *sanchita karma*, and thus it goes on.

THE WHEEL OF KARMA

Unable to liberate ourselves from our own karma, we find ourselves ruthlessly trapped by our own actions. We consult astrologers and palmists to know of our future, little realising that it is our past and present actions that determine our future! Even while we are exhausting our *prarabdha karma*, we are adding to our store of *sanchita karma*, for we continue to sow the seeds of karma anew! Our *sanchita karma* keeps growing, and we live in ignorance of this inescapable truth!

Our *sanchita karma* keeps on multiplying by leaps and bounds. It is not possible for us to exhaust it entirely. And so we are mercilessly bound to this wheel of karma, this wheel of birth and death.

The effect of *prarabdha karma* is inescapable, no matter how hard we try to evade its consequences. Only two choices are open to us – to accept whatever happens in a spirit of faith, and to bear it cheerfully; or to resist it, protest against our fate and spend our life in misery. We cannot change our *prarabdha karma* – but we can, in fact we must change our attitude to life.

The question then arises: is there a way out for us?

The wheel of birth and death is not a wheel of eternal happiness! We are only too well aware that while we get a little pleasure, we also undergo a great deal of agony, anguish, misery and suffering. At such times, we cry for relief: Is there a way out? How may we be freed once and for all, from this load of karma?

FREEDOM THROUGH DIVINE GRACE

We have said that we are bound by the law of karma, and that our personality, our present life, and even our *swabhava* or nature, are determined by our past karma. This will make you wonder whether your own effort or voluntary action has anything to do with your liberation. After all, if everything is predetermined, what is the use of human effort?

Prarabdha represents only the broad outline of our present life. While this is given, certain scholars argue, *purushartha* or self-effort can always help you improve upon this broad outline.

For example, if *prarabdha* has made you wealthy and prosperous in this life, you will waste it all away if you remain idle or complacent, simply revelling in the worldly pleasures. On the other hand, if you cultivate humility and compassion through your self-effort, you are actually improving upon your *prarabdha*. You will then give freely to the poor and the needy, and devote your God-given wealth to the service of your fellow human beings. Thus, you are ensuring that your past good karma is actually being converted to good karma for your future!

The ancient scriptures of India tell us that there are four objectives for self-effort – four purposes of life. These have been identified as *dharma, artha, kama* and *moksha*.

Dharma represents the ethical principles of right living. These moral values should form the basis of all our actions. If our actions are unethical or immoral, all that we achieve in life will have no real meaning or value. For example, a society or a nation, which believes only in material progress at any cost, is likely to disintegrate with moral degeneration. Thus *dharma* must be the basis of all our self-effort.

Artha represents material values. Our ancestors did not overlook the importance of material security. We must strive in order to have the means for our livelihood; we do not have to be millionaires, but we must have enough means to fulfil all the duties that *dharma* demands of us.

Kama represents the vital value of desire. *Kama* motivates us to make friends, to marry and start a family, to relate to the people around us. Within the bounds of *dharma*, *kama* can lead to a life of joyous fulfilment.

However, all these values – *dharma*, *artha* and *kama* are but means to an end. The ultimate goal of human life is *moksha* or liberation – and this requires untiring, unfailing, persistent self-effort from us. Liberation is not determined by destiny; liberation cannot be predicted by astrology or palmistry. Liberation is achieved only through self-effort and the grace of God or the guru.

In this process, you will need the guidance of a guru, whose moral support can help you on the path. Self-effort is necessary to surrender your will to the guru, and to pursue the path with faith and devotion.

When you follow the right direction, you will soon realise that you are being drawn towards divine grace. Your self-effort has led you to this beautiful state, which is the ultimate aim of human life.

Many people are often confused about the balance between self-effort and divine grace. What is the dividing line between the two? Does self-effort cease when divine grace operates?

All of us know divine grace sustains our life. Yet none of us can sit still before a plate of food and wait for divine grace to bring the food to our lips!

When there is something that we desire intensely – like the first rank in class, the first prize in a contest, or a girl/boy we love – we put in every effort to secure the object of that desire. When we encounter obstacles in our path, we invoke divine grace. When we don't get what we want, we deny the mercy of God.

This is not the right attitude: as the saying goes, God helps those who help themselves. God's grace operates through your own mind, intellect and heart. God's grace guides your every effort, though you may be unaware of it. As you strive to do the best you can, divine grace prompts you, supports you at every step.

Our scriptures distinguish four aspects of divine grace: *Ishwara kripa, Guru kripa, Shastra kripa* and *Sva kripa.*

Ishwara kripa is the divine assistance that comes to our aid when all else fails us. Consider the plight of Draupadi, as she was about to be disgraced, dishonoured, derobed by the Kauravas. All earthly sources of help failed Draupadi utterly, in her hour of desperate, piteous need.

However, Draupadi knew that there was One whose grace is unfailing. One, whose support is perennial. Therefore, she called upon Sri Krishna. He came to her aid promptly. We have all benefited from *Ishwara kripa* in our lives, though circumstances might not have been so dramatic.

Guru kripa or the grace of the guru, is the amazing protection that the guru offers to his disciples. When we surrender ourselves to his will utterly and completely, the guru's guidance is made available to us at every step.

Shastra kripa, the grace of the scriptures, is not obtained merely by reading the words or the pages of the sacred texts. It is when you approach the scriptures in the right frame of mind, with the right attitude, and eager to assimilate their truth, that their essential meaning is revealed to you. When you internalise the truth of the texts you read – and not merely quote or recite from them – you have reached a crucial stage in your spiritual development.

Sva kripa or the grace of your own soul enables you to take a deep interest in spiritual matters. You are not distracted by materialistic goals. Worldly affairs do not take you away from the chosen path to God; you are not tempted by the passing shadows of life. The grace of the soul enables you to pursue the pilgrim-path with patience and perseverance.

If we are to receive divine grace, we must learn to become willing receptacles of the same. This is possible through *sadhana* or spiritual discipline.

Sadhana too, is a matter of self-effort. This becomes possible, when we notice the ever-loving presence of God in our lives, and surrender ourselves to this grace. Therefore, we appreciate the crucial interdependence between our effort and His grace.

WHAT IS FATE?

Que sera, sera…Whatever will be will be…

The lines of the popular song express the popular view of fate. "It is in the stars," we say, shifting responsibility to astrology. "It is written thus on my brow," we remark, absolving ourselves of all accountability.

True, it is fate that governs your future – but it is you who create your own destiny. You ordain your own fate, by the law of cause and effect.

God has given us the freedom to choose, the freedom to act. But we are responsible for the outcome of our own choices and actions. Thus every choice we make, every act we perform becomes a cause that will produce an effect that will determine our fate and our future.

Disease or good health; success or failure; poverty or wealth; all these are the effects of causes we have created in our past. However, we can change the effect on our fate if we choose the right way through right action.

Let's see this example, when a person is afflicted with a heart problem, he bemoans his fate. If only he would look carefully at his actions, he will understand he has been eating the wrong kind of food, leading the wrong kind of lifestyle and choosing bad habits over good ones. A bad lifestyle was the cause; the heart problem is the effect. He himself has created his 'fate'.

When we are ill, we go to a doctor. This is one way to *minimise, mitigate* the bad effects of our illness. However, when the disease is deep-rooted, the underlying cause has to be eliminated.

One way to change fate is to *resist* the effects of our causes. Thus, when we are confronted by trouble, we can affirm our belief in the goodness of God, in the positive forces of health and happiness. In such a state of mind, the negative conditions will affect you far less than they otherwise would.

A third way to control your fate is to *break* the hold that fate has on you, to *stop* its bad effects completely. This involves a process like surgery, when a diseased organ is removed from our body.

Never give up your good efforts. They will definitely help you change, resist, even stop your karma. You truly will become the master of your own Fate.

PRACTICAL SUGGESTIONS

How may we live a life that bears witness to the law of karma? How may we avoid adding to our karmic load and create good karma for ourselves?

Let me pass on to you a few suggestions that can be helpful in daily life:

1. Always be aware of your thoughts. A thought is power; it

is energy. As you think, so you become. Every time an evil thought approaches you, push it out of your mind. An effective way of pushing out a bad thought is to slap or pinch yourself the moment an undesirable thought enters your mind.

2. As you sow, so shall you reap. Therefore, be aware of every little thing that you do. Every day, spend some time in silence, preferably at the same time and at the same place. Sitting in silence, go over all that you did during the earlier twenty four hours. It is helpful if you go over your actions in the reverse order – think first of what you did a little while ago, then of what you did some time earlier, and so on. You will surely find that there were things which you did which you should not have done, as there are things which you did not do but should have done – many errors of commission and omission. Repent for them all and pray to the Lord for wisdom and strength to never to do such things again.

3. Take care of your *sanga* – the people with whom you associate. If you move in the company of holy ones, something of their holiness will penetrate your life and fill you with holy aspirations and vibrations. Hence the value of daily *satsang*.

4. Develop the spirit of detachment. Attend to your duties but be inwardly detached, knowing that nothing, nobody belongs to you. You are only an actor – but also a spectator – in the ever unfolding, cosmic drama of life. You have to learn to play this double role of an actor and a spectator.

5. Grow in the spirit of surrender to God, "Not my will, but Thy Will be done, O Lord!" Repeat the Name Divine, and pray with a sincere heart that you may rise above the *dwandas* (the pairs of opposites), above pleasure and pain, loss and gain, for it is only then that suffering will not be able to touch you – and you shall be at peace with yourself and with those around you.

6. Be vigilant. Be watchful, live in awareness all the time. The

Buddha said to his disciples on one occasion, "O *bhikkhus*, if you are not vigilant, desire will enter your heart even as rain enters a room through a leaky roof."

7. Do as much good as you can, to as many as you can, in as many ways as you can. Help as many as you can, to lift the load on the rough road of life. The day on which we have not helped a brother here, a sister there, a bird here, an animal there, is a lost day, indeed.

KARMA – FAQ's

Q: How does bad karma originate?

A: Man was given free will, He was given the right of choice. He can choose between what the Upanishads call *preya* and *shreya*. *Preya* is the pleasant: the path of *preya* is the path of pleasure that lures us but leads us to our degradation.

Shreya is the good: the path of *shreya* may, at first, be difficult to tread; but ultimately it leads to our betterment, well-being and spiritual unfolding. At every step man is given this choice. Many of us, alas, choose the easy path – the path of pleasure – and so we keep on multiplying undesirable karma.

Q: Can our bad karma be mitigated or lessened? Is there any hope for us?

A: Evil karma can be mitigated or lessened by *nama japa* and selfless service to those that suffer and are in pain, and above all, through the grace of God or a Godman.

Q: In the law of evolution, can a human being be reborn as an animal?

A: When the law of karma finds that a person is so incorrigible that he will not be reformed until he goes back to the stage of the animal, and begins again – it is only in such cases that a human being is reborn as an animal.

I sometimes think about a classmate of mine. When I was in the first standard, he was in the fourth. I came to the second, he was still in the fourth standard. He continued failing till I went to the fifth and the teacher said, "We must do something. This boy has been in the fourth standard for so many years, let us send him back to the third, so that he can gather some momentum."

I do not feel that anyone of you could have had that experience.

But it does happen in very few cases, where people commit mortal crimes, for example killing little children. Then perhaps, the law of karma gives us the body of an animal so that we can restart the process. But it is always for our own good.

Q: Why are our past karmas kept a secret from us?

A: Don't you think it is a great mercy of God that our karmic links are not known to us? Else, it may be difficult for us to live in this world. Thus, for instance, there may be a man whose wife was his bitter enemy in an earlier incarnation and has now become his wife only to settle previous accounts. If all this were revealed to us, what would be our condition?

Q: If all that happens today is the result of our past karma, does it mean that everything is predestined?

A: No, certainly not! We are the architects of our own destiny, the builders of our own future. Many of us blame fate, or *kismet* for our misfortunes. But let me tell you, that you are the builders of your own fate. Therefore, be careful, especially, of your thoughts. We pay scant attention to our thoughts, believing them to be of no consequence. We say, after all, it was only a thought, what does it matter? Every thought is a seed you are sowing in the field of life. What you sow today, you will have to reap in the near or remote future.

God has created a universe of beauty, fullness, happiness and harmony. Each one of us is a child of God. God wishes each one of us to be happy, prosperous, successful and to enjoy all the good things He has created. We keep ourselves away from all these bounties because of our karma. Change your karma and you will change the condition in which you live. And you can change your karma by adopting a new pattern of thinking.

Q: Can karmas be wiped off by *japa*?

A: It is believed that the effects of karma can be mitigated through *nama japa*. In any case, the suffering can be reduced, because *nama japa* acts as a sort of chloroform. It is like going through an operation, where the surgeon puts you under anaesthesia and you come out of the surgery without feeling the acute pain. Otherwise the pain is so excruciating, that a person could die of it. This is what *nama japa* does to you.

Q: Can saints take over the karma of their disciples?

A: They can. However, normally, they do not wish to interfere with the law of karma. For they know that the law of karma does not wish to punish us for what we may have done in the past. The law of karma wishes to reform us and so sends us experiences which may help in our spiritual advancement. It is true there have been cases when men of God have taken the karmas of their devotees upon themselves. It is like buying birds and setting them free. Likewise, a man who is rich in the wealth of the Spirit may, if he so desires, pay for our karma and release us from the cage of *maya*.

Q: Does man get *mukti* (liberation from the cycle of birth and death) after working out his karma?

A: Karma leads to karma, the process of sowing and reaping goes on endlessly. But *mukti*, liberation, comes through the grace of God. Thus we have cases of sinners being suddenly transformed into saints. It was a Christian saint who said, "What God is by nature, man becomes by grace." Through grace, man becomes Godlike, emancipated, free!

Q: Is there no shortcut to the ending of karma?

A: Yes. There are three ways. The first is the way of self-inquiry, to understand who you are. You are not the body, nor the mind. You are not the *buddhi*. You are that which cannot be touched by karma. Once you arrive at that stage all karma drops out.

The other is the way of self-surrender.

The third is the way of selfless service.

Those are the three ways by which the store of karma can be burnt. But even then, the *prarabdha karma* (fructified karma) that you have brought with you into this life, has to be worked out. But the *sanchita karma*, the storehouse of karma, gets burnt.

Q: Don't you think it is very difficult for young people to accept these three points?

A: In that case we have to keep entering the cycle of birth and death, until it becomes easy for us to do it. Experience teaches us. We have to pass through those experiences. Very few learn through vicarious experiences.

A parent says to the child, "My child, never do this. I did this and I repented." The child will not understand. He would like to do that and, from his own experience, learn what it is to repent after doing a particular thing. But there are some who learn from vicarious experience.

This worldly life is a prison; and in this prison, we are bound by *maya*, worldly illusion. We are prisoners. We think we are free but we are in bondage. We need to be liberated. To get *mukti*, you need *mumukshatwa*, the desire, the intense longing, for liberation. That is very necessary. Until that arises, you don't want to be liberated. You are happy and satisfied with whatever life gives you.

There was a man. They asked him, "Why don't you desire to go to heaven?" He said, "Life must be boring there. Here it is exciting."

How can a person with such an attitude ever aspire to, leave alone attain Liberation?

Q: If everything that happens to us is ordained by God, then how are we responsible for our actions?

A: So long as man has the egoistic feeling in his mind that he is the doer, he is responsible for his own actions.

When he frees himself from the ego, transcends this feeling of doing, he becomes an instrument of God and all the responsibility for his actions belong to God.

Q: How do we know in any situation that it is God's Will taking effect and not our will?

A: There are certain things that happen to us. We do not want them to happen and try to avoid or escape them. But in spite of all our efforts, things happen. Those are the things that we should accept as God's Will. It is something that I did not want to happen yet it has happened. But there are other things that I do, for which I will be held responsible.

Q: Tell us how to face suffering?

A: If our attention is on suffering, it gets magnified beyond all proportions. In the midst of suffering let us count our blessings. Usually, we suffer only in one area of our life. There are so many other things for which we should be grateful. Take a piece of paper and make a list of all the blessings you still have. There was a man who started from scratch and built up a flourishing business and one day became bankrupt. The first thing he did was to take a piece of paper and write down all the things he still possessed. He found, he still had a great deal to be thankful for. With gratitude in his heart, he started anew and built up a still larger business. If we count our blessings, our suffering recedes in the background.

Let us make it a habit – to praise the Lord at every step, in every round of life. Even in the midst of fear and frustrations, worry and anxiety, depression and disappointment, don't stop chanting His Name. When we thank the Lord all the time, we build for ourselves a ladder of consciousness on which we can climb and touch the very pinnacle of peace.

Let me tell you the story of a woman. Her husband fell seriously ill. The doctor despaired of his condition and said he would not be able to last longer than six months. The woman had deep faith in God and started thanking the Lord a thousand times every day. "Thank you, God! Thank you, God!" she prayed again and again.

Strangely enough, a few months later, when the husband went for a checkup, the doctors were amazed at his miraculous recovery. "A power above and beyond ours, has been at work!" they exclaimed. In every situation, do the very best you can and leave the result to the Lord. When Henry Ford was 75 years old, he was asked the secret of his success. He answered: "My life is built in these three rules. I do not eat too much, I do not worry too much and, if I do my best, I believe that what happens, happens for the best."

NEW AGE KARMA

I received an anonymous letter written by someone who was

present at one of my discourses on karma. In the course of the letter he writes: "Your talk outlines no new approach to the problem."

I confess I am not a scholar. I am not qualified to give intellectual interpretations. I do aspire to give life – interpretations. The law of karma is an eternal law: it is a universal law. It needs to be interpreted in life. Therefore, as I said, I am interested in a life-interpretation of this and other eternal laws.

I recall having read many years ago, concerning an eminent Confucian scholar. He was 80 years of age, and it was believed that no one could equal him in China in learning and understanding. One day he learnt that far, far away a new doctrine had sprung up that was profoundly deeper than his knowledge. This upset him. He lost his interest in life. He decided that the issue must be decided one way or the other. He undertook a long journey, traversed many miles and met the master of the new Zen school. He asked him to explain the new doctrine.

The Buddhist philosophy is simple and can be summed up in one sentence, "To avoid doing evil, to do as much good as possible, this is the teaching of all the Buddhas." That means to bring out the Buddha in each one of us.

On hearing this, the old Confucian scholar flared up and said: "What do you mean? I have come here facing the dangers and hazards of a long, perilous journey in spite of my advanced age. And you just quote a little jingle that every three-year-old child knows by heart! Are you mocking me?" The Zen master very politely answered: "I am not mocking you. But please consider that though every three-year-old child knows these words by heart, yet even a man of eighty fails to live up to them!"

It is life that is needed, not doctrines, creeds or dogmas. Do we bear witness to the great teachings in deeds of daily living?

Yes, it is life that is needed, not book learning, nor intellectual or psychological interpretations. Our friend writes in his beautiful letter that there is exploitation everywhere: exploitation and social injustice and suffering are due to the fact that we have not learnt to interpret the law of karma in our daily life. If we truly believed in the law of karma, there would be no exploitation, for the law of karma boldly declares: "He that exploits shall be exploited." If India is to be made new, what is needed is not new interpretations but translation of the teachings in our daily lives.

Only a few days ago, I visited a sick woman. She is not learned in the lore of books. She had a severe backache, excruciating pain at the base of the spine. She could neither sit nor stand, neither bend nor walk. Despite it all, there was a smile on her face as she said to me: "I must have done something during one of my earlier births to deserve this condition. Perhaps, I have beaten someone on the back with a stick. God save me from doing any evil in this birth."

This is the prayer of everyone who believes in the law of karma: "God save me from doing any evil!" And if this becomes the prayer of every man and woman in India, this ancient, unhappy land will become new and India will shine, once again, in the splendour of the new morning sun.

Live and move and do your daily work in the ever living presence of God!

This was the teaching that was given to every student in ancient India. There is an oft-repeated story of a guru and two disciples who came to him seeking admission to the *ashrama*. The guru gives them a coconut each and instructs them to break the coconut where no one may see them, and return with the broken pieces. One of the students enters a dark and solitary cave and, finding no one watching, breaks the coconut and within no time, returns to the *ashrama*. The second disciple returns only after sunset and that, too, with the coconut intact. His friend says to him: "Why did you not accompany me? There were so many caves. I entered one of them. You could have entered another and broken the coconut. Nobody would have seen you." At this, the other friend replies: "I entered cave after cave, but wherever I went, just as I was about to break the coconut, I found that He was watching me. God was watching me! There was not a nook or a corner where God was not!"

How many of us live in this consciousness? This is an ancient interpretation of an ancient, eternal law. But how many live up to it?

> Be careful little eyes what you see:
> There's a Father up above,
> Watching you in love,
> So be careful little eyes what you see!
> Be careful little ears what you hear:
> There's a Father up above,
> Watching you in love,
> So be careful little ears what you hear!
> Be careful little tongue what you speak:
> There's a Father up above,
> Watching you in love,
> So be careful little tongue what you speak!
> Be careful little hands what you do:
> There's a Father up above,
> Watching you in love,
> So be careful little hands what you do!
> Be careful little feet where you go:
> There's a Father up above,
> Watching you in love,
> So be careful little feet where you go!
> Be careful little mind what you think:

There's a Father up above,
Watching you in love,
So be careful little mind what you think!
Be careful little heart what you feel:
There's a Father up above,
Watching you in love,
So be careful little heart what you feel!

SPIRITUALITY IN DAILY LIFE

WHAT IS SPIRITUALITY?

The Sanskrit term for spirituality is *atma vidya*, which literally means 'the science of the spirit'. Spirituality, I feel, is also a science. It is concerned with the quest for truth. It is a process of experimentation leading to a great discovery – the discovery of the self.

Spirituality begins with the quest to know the self; and this quest is endless in itself. Since the dawn of civilization, men of thought have grappled with such questions as: Who am I? Where do I come from? Where am I going? What is the purpose for which I was made? How may I fulfill that purpose?

Spirituality is in many ways a quest to find answers to these questions.

A guru was addressing a group of his disciples in his serene and quiet *ashrama* on the banks of the river Yamuna. "The spark of the divine is within you, you are an aspect of the divine. You must constantly aspire for perfection; to be perfect is to be Godlike."

One of the disciples was puzzled by the remark. He stood up and said to the guru, "But sire, God is great. He is Omnipotent, Omnipresent and Omniscient. Infinite worlds exist within Him. How can we ever hope to be like God?"

The guru said to him, "Here is my water bowl. Take it to the Yamuna river and fill it with water." The disciple left and in a few minutes he was back with a filled bowl. The guru looked at the bowl and said, "This is not the water from the Yamuna. I told you to get water from the Yamuna river."

"I beg your pardon, Guruji," said the disciple. "This is water from the Yamuna river. I did exactly what you told me to do."

"I tell you, this cannot be water from the Yamuna," insisted the guru. "There are fish and turtles in the Yamuna; there are cows standing in the river; there are people bathing in its waters.

Where are the fish in this bowl? Where are the turtles and cows? Why, there isn't a single person bathing here! And you tell me this is the water of the Yamuna river? Go and get me the water of the Yamuna river."

The disciple was taken aback. "But Guruji," he stammered. "I brought just a bowl full of water from the Yamuna for you. How can a bowl contain all those things you mention?"

"True, a little bowl can't contain all those things," agreed the guru. "Now go and pour this water back into the Yamuna."

The disciple went and poured the water into the river, and returned.

"Tell me, don't all those things exist in the water now?" the guru asked him. "See for yourself, the fish, the turtles, the cows and the people; they are all in the river, aren't they? The individual soul is like the water in the bowl. It is one with God, but it exists in a limited form, and therefore it seems to be very different from God. When you poured the water from the bowl back into the river, that water once again contained fish, turtles, cows and everything else that the river contains. In the same way, when you see your own inner self through meditation and knowledge, you will realise that you are 'That' and that your spirit pervades everywhere, just like God. Once you are aware of this, you will know that you are an aspect of God!"

In simple terms, spirituality is knowledge of God, not an intellectual knowledge but an illumined personal experience of the Supreme. Our spiritual hearts are blotted with many stains. They are not pure. We need to purify them.

God is the goal of life. To move Godward, we need to get up and open the door and let God in. This happens only when man recognises the need for God. Out of the very depths of his heart, there awakes the cry: "I have need of You, Lord! I cannot live without You!" This is known as 'spiritual awakening'. Something happens deep within you and your life becomes new. You are filled with light and warmth, joy and peace.

THE QUEST FOR SPIRITUALITY

The Sufi masters tell us that there are three journeys on the road to self-realisation:

1. During the first journey man wanders endlessly and his wanderings lead him away from truth. His restless mind, led by the senses, leads man to seek all the pleasures of the world and he gets caught in worldly affairs, forgetting the purpose of his journey, the goal of his life. This is the journey that most of us are currently pursuing!

2. The second journey begins with the awakening of the soul. It begins with the awareness that we have to return to our true home, back to where we came from. We begin to question the worth and value of all that we have achieved in worldly terms. "There must be more to life than this!" is the one thought that impels us at this stage.

3. The third journey follows as a logical consequence to the second. We realise that we have wandered from our path. We make the crucial U-turn that will take us back to God. God is our source and origin: He is also the destination of our earthly journey. He is the Ultimate goal of our life. Now begins our serious, persistent search for God.

The first journey may be the result of an unheeding, unaware attitude; the second journey is the dawn of true awareness; and the third and final journey must always be a conscious, deliberate exercise, undertaken of our own free will and the effort to translate that will into reality. It is a journey towards self-awareness! But it is not the end! For I believe that there is a fourth and final journey which represents the ultimate: it is the journey within the self, within God.

Let me illustrate this with a story from the Buddhist scriptures.

An elderly grandmother once approached the Buddha and told him that she longed to live a spiritual life; but she was too old and frail to withstand the rigors of monastic living; and her household chores were so tedious and time consuming that she could not set aside enough time to meditate. "What can I do?" she wailed.

"Respected grandmother," replied the Buddha, "every time you draw water from the well for your family, remain aware of every movement and motion of your hands and wrists. As you carry the water jug on your head, be aware of every step that your feet take; as you attend to the chores in your kitchen, maintain continuous mindfulness moment after moment. You too, will discover the art of Meditation."

Spirituality is unique and different for each one of us, because our souls are at different stages of evolution towards ultimate self-knowledge and liberation.

Liberation or *moksha* is the ultimate goal of life, according to Hinduism. The easiest way to attain this goal, step by step, is to do good karma and avoid bad karma.

God 'pierced' us with five senses so that they are constantly tuned to the outer reality; but the senses can be controlled, so that the mind and consciousness can be focused within. Spirituality is thus a discipline; essentially, self-discipline.

We can safely believe that spirituality is not the same as the following:

1. Spirituality is not the same as religion.
2. Spirituality is not a rite or ritual.
3. It is not a set of practices.
4. It is not meant exclusively for (a) the old, (b) the wise, (c) the religiously devout, (d) the superintelligent or (e) the *jnani* or the evolved ones.
5. It is not asceticism or renunciation, though some people have chosen them as preferred modes to attain self-knowledge.

Through this process of negation, we arrive at what spirituality is all about: although I must emphasise, it is different for each one of us:

1. It is a quest for self-discovery and emphasises the inter connectedness of all creation.
2. It is discovering the divine within you – and within all creation.
3. It is a desire to transcend the ego, its limitations, its fears and insecurities.
4. It is the knowledge that I and my fellow human beings and my fellow creatures are part of the One Whole.
5. It is discovering the power of love, compassion and respect – nay, reverence for all forms of life.
6. At its best, it is Yoga – union with God.

For me as an individual, it is easy to detach spirituality from religion, but not from God! I do believe that atheists and agnostics can also be deeply spiritual in their own way. But for me, spirituality is man's quest for God.

We once asked Gurudev Sadhu Vaswani, "What is the beginning of the spiritual life?" Gurudev's answer was clear and precise. "When I lose myself, I find the Soul."

Finding your soul – that is the essence of spirituality. It is the aspiration, the genuine effort to know our true self. It begins with the cognizance that we are not the bodies we wear; the body is only a garment we have worn during this present earth incarnation. The more we identify with the body, the more we get entangled in *maya*.

Once upon a time, there lived a wise and holy sage who had attained spiritual illumination. Many were eager to see him, speak to him and be blessed by him. Whenever there was a knock at his door, he would ask, "Who are you?" The visitor would invariably say, "I am so-and-so."

"Why have you come?" the sage would ask next.

"O holy one, give me your blessings so that…" and the visitors would place their desires before the holy one. "So that I can have a rich harvest…", "So that I may have a son…" and so on.

Receiving such answers, the sage would lapse into silence. He would not open the door. Thus many people came to him and went away disappointed.

One day, a seeker came to knock at the holy man's door.

"Who are you?" called out the sage.

"I wish I knew," came the answer. "Oh holy one, I beg you to enlighten me, for I don't know who I am, and why I came into this world. Please show me the way, so that I may attain the true goal of this, my human life."

The holy man was pleased with this reply and opened his door to admit the seeker. He realized that the man was a genuine aspirant, thirsting for the truth. He took him as his disciple, and initiated him on the path of self-realisation.

The soul, the *atman*, the indwelling one, passes from body

to body. It is unaffected by outer things. The Self abides: the bodies are transient.

The Lord tells Arjuna: "You have always been; you will always be." This is the awareness that we must try to attain – that we are immortal, that we abide in Eternity. Therefore, do not become a slave of the body.

Tat twam asi! That art Thou! In the *Mundaka Upanishad*, we are told of two birds perched on the branches of the selfsame tree. One of them is always looking up at the sky; it is ecstatic, energetic and sings a song of divine beauty. The other bird, perched on a lower branch, glances downwards, and is overwhelmed by anguish and misery.

The two birds symbolise the Self – the first, which looks upward, has discovered the essential glory of the divine self within. The second is attached to the body, to the earth, and is weighed down by attachment and grief.

The guru will unfold to our consciousness the truth that inside each one of us is *Sat-chit-ananda* – true, eternal, blissful knowledge.

Identification with the body, egoism and ignorance of the true nature of the self – these three are identified by sages as the cause of all human suffering. Egoism can only be removed by the purification of the mind and the senses.

I will share with you a five-fold teaching that I received in my youth from an unknown saint. These lessons taught me to move away, gradually, from identifying myself with the body:

- Remember, that you are a pilgrim here, a wayfarer in quest of your lost homeland. Your Home is in Eternity.
- Be patient in the midst of the difficulties and dangers of life.

Remind yourself again and again, "This too shall pass!"
- Each day meditate on death, for death approaches us with each passing moment.
- Give the service of love to all.
- Seek fellowship with saints and holy men so that the tiny drop that you are may become a mighty ocean.

WHY DO WE NEED TO BE SPIRITUAL?

All of us subsist on a physical plane; we cannot do without the basic needs; we crave for more wealth, more possessions, more acquisitions; but the intelligent ones among us know that wealth and possessions cannot really make us happy. We are fascinated by the rare moments in our life when we are filled with awe, wonder and a sense of mystery that send our spirits soaring. We know that none of these finer feelings can be captured by a materialistic way of life!

In the past, the distinction between spirituality and the workaday world was so sharp that people renounced the world and worldly activities to contemplate on the higher things of life. But today, the boundaries have blurred.

All of us are concerned about our inner life; we all crave for a sense of peace and harmony that is central to our being. We may not want to renounce the world to find that elusive peace; but we are ready and willing to spend some time focussing our attention on the rich interior world that is within us.

Spirituality, like faith, is a very personal concept. Atheists deny it; agnostics speculate about it in a detached manner; I do believe that there are thousands of people who practice some form of spirituality in their daily lives – through inner reflection, contemplation or even through silence and service – without actually codifying their behaviour. In this sense, spirituality is a means to an end; and this 'end' or 'goal' may also vary from person to person. In our Hindu way of thinking, the highest goal is the goal of Liberation – freedom from the eternal cycle of birth, death, rebirth.

The purpose of human birth is to free ourselves from this vicious cycle. Freedom is breaking away from bad habits, addictions and wrong attitudes; freedom is conquering the lower self; freedom is the ability to rise to the highest level of consciousness and the purest level of thought that we, as human beings, are capable of! It is this level, this height of awareness that we reach when we follow Sri Krishna's profoundly simple, yet powerful advice in the Gita: "Whatever you do, whatever you eat or pray, do it as an offering unto Me!"

Spirituality is as simple as this: let all our thoughts and words and deeds be an offering unto the Lord!

One of the reasons why we do not connect with God is because God has not become real to us. To many of us, God is a distant being. True, God dwells in the heavens above, but there is not a nook, not a corner on the earth, where He does not dwell. Alas, many of us do not feel His presence.

What we need is the rediscovery of the great truth that God is – that He is real; that we need to renew our faith in Him.

Let us take out a little Personal Quiet Time (PQT) for ourselves every day.

In silence, let us pray, meditate, repeat the Name Divine, do our spiritual thinking, engage ourselves in a loving and intimate conversation with God.

Once your insights are clear, you need to translate them into deeds of daily life: into good thoughts, good words and good deeds.

A few suggestions for bringing Spirituality in our daily lives:

1. Begin the day with God!

The first thing we do on getting up in the morning shapes the entire day. Choose the right thing to begin your day.

2. Leave off fretting and worrying about every little problem. Leave it to God to take care of you and the others.

Put God first. He will automatically free us from our worries, and take care of all our 'concerns' and 'problems'. There is a beautiful line in the Sukhmani Sahib, a Sikh Scripture which I love to meditate on:

Avar tyag tu tisay chitar...

Renounce everything; throw out everything; don't think of anything– but meditate on Him; i.e. concentrate on Him; think of Him, dedicate all your work to Him!

3. Count Your Blessings!

Should we not feel grateful to God for the innumerable gifts He has bestowed on us; two eyes with which to see the beauty of the world around us, two ears with which to hear music, song, conversation and children's laughter; two hands with which to do a thousand things; two feet which can take us wherever we choose to walk... And that is not all. He has given us people who love us – family, brothers and sisters, friends and well-wishers!

4. Accept God's Will!

Wisdom consists in accepting God's Will – not with despair or resignation, but in peace and faith, knowing that our journey through life has been perfectly planned by Infinite love and Infinite wisdom. There can be no mistake in God's plan for us!

5. Do your best – and leave the rest to God.

Work is worship. But the secret of inner peace is to work without attachment to the results.

6. Seek not power! Seek service!

Let us do as much good as we can, to as many as we can, in as many ways as we can, whenever we can and as long as we can!

God is Absolute Love – and if we love God, we must be imbued with the longing to serve our fellow men. Let us give with love and compassion, and we will make the world a better place to live in!

SADHANA FOR SEEKERS OF THE SPIRIT

Sadhana is a spiritual discipline which is essential for all seekers of truth. But, as we may appreciate, every seeker after truth is different. Therefore, there are several *sadhanas* or techniques available to the seeker on the path of spiritual growth. We can take to prayer; we can take to *pooja* or organised ritual worship; we can choose *dhyana* or meditation; we can choose *japa yoga*, *Naam smaran* – remembering the Lord's Name is one of the simplest and most effective.

Why should we practise *sadhana*? What will we get out of it?

There is a simple input output ratio that operates in *sadhana*; you will get as much out of it as you put into it! Put faith and perseverance: and you will achieve your goal – indeed, you will achieve much more than you expect, with the grace of God.

Let us look at a few *sadhanas* mentioned earlier:

Prayer

Simply put, prayer is turning to God. At its most mystic, prayer is stopping the current of your worldly life to give a few moments to God exclusively!

Meditation

For many meditation is a difficult art, though it is quite simple. Meditation is directing our attention to the Eternal and keeping it there for a while. When we do so, we become conscious of infinite power, a wondrous peace.

Naam Smaran

Think of God in any form that draws you. He is the Formless One, but for the sake of His devotees, He has worn many forms.

Call Him by any name that appeals to you. He is the Nameless One, though the sages have called Him by many Names. Do not quarrel over forms or names.

All forms and names ultimately lead to the One who is beyond the form and the formlessness. "On whatever path men approach Me," says the Lord in the Gita, "on that I go to meet them – for all the paths are Mine, verily Mine!"

Mantra Jaap

A mantra is a sacred utterance. In Hinduism, it is a sacred verbal formula repeated in prayer, meditation or incantation. A mantra is a word or a combination of words which have great power. It helps you to concentrate your wandering mind.

Pranayama

The meaning of *pranayama* is explained thus: *prana* means "life force or energy" and *yama* means "control of that energy."

Pranayama is "extension or expansion" of the flow of energy. Deep breathing brings immense benefits to us, including a stable mind, steady thinking, inner peace, good health and a longer life.

We may see that the Gita talks of different paths to attain the Supreme Reality:

1. Comprehension of the Supreme Reality through Rational Understanding.
2. Concentration on the Supreme Reality through Meditation.
3. Performing actions that are dedicated to God.
4. Performing actions selflessly – without expectation of results.
5. Single-minded devotion to God.

The message of the Gita is the message of courage, heroism and *atma shakti*. It is this *shakti* that we need to overcome despair, doubt and pessimism on the spiritual path. The Gita teaches us that weakness is a sin, while *shakti* is a spiritual virtue.

The Gita's message is not for meditation alone; it is for deeds of daily life; it is for action; it is for you and me.

Gurudev Sadhu Vaswani urged us to study and follow the norms and the spiritual regimen strictly. He said:

> By merely jumping into the ocean
> You do not get oysters with pearls,
> Dive deep into the ocean,
> Dive tirelessly and you will find,
> The invaluable treasure of pearls that you seek.

Is this not true of all human endeavours?

Walk the path of the spiritual seeker, and you will be amazed by all the benefits you reap, here in this workaday world!

1. You will discover your higher self – the self that you were not really aware of.

2. You will understand that life is a joyous, blessed journey, when you have set for yourself the goal of spiritual evolution.

3. You will discover a subtle change in your perspective that makes you realise that the world is not what you had imagined it to be – an arena of strife and defeat and struggle and pain.

4. In a very subtle way too, you will find yourself taking charge of your own life, becoming the master rather than the slave of your circumstances.

5. With your changing attitude and new perception, you will rediscover the magic, the wonder that is life. You will take nothing for granted.

6. The spirit of gratitude and thanksgiving that this leads you to, will itself transform your life.

7. You will find that walking the path of the seeker will give you a new sense of balance, that enables you to take on joy and sorrow, and all those vicissitudes of life with an evenhand.

8. You will attain to that inner peace and harmony, that is greater than all the wealth of this world. It will not be threatened by adverse changes in your external circumstances.

9. You will discover a new sense of purpose in living your life to the fullest, giving, sharing, caring, supporting, sympathising and offering your hand of help and healing to all who come in contact with you.

10. You will discover the tremendous joy and peace that

are to be found in solitude and silence. You will find too, that in silence and solitude, you draw ever closer to God. You will realise that you are not alone – that God is ever with you, guiding you, guarding you, watching over you and protecting you with His loving grace.

11. Blessed by the showers of His love and grace, you will find yourself radiating love and peace all around you.

12. You will grow in inner strength and faith – the triple faith in yourself, in the universe and in God, which is the key to a truly meaningful life that is well lived in every sense of the term!

THE TIME TO BEGIN IS NOW!

Every one of us understands that there is more to this life than accumulating wealth, and attaining success. On the one hand, we know in our heart of hearts that we must make the most of this precious life; on the other we are only too well aware that this life is transient. To live a life that is pure, beautiful, selfless; and offered as an *ahuti* for the glory of God – it is the *sadhana* of daily life, living life as it ought to be lived!

Man is known by the company he keeps. Man certainly has a choice here. The company of the good and virtuous ones or company that makes him miserable and loathsome.

"The Soul selects her own society," sang a woman poet. Such an association nourishes and sustains our spiritual evolution. Such is the environment offered to all of us in the *satsang*.

The external environment has profound effect on both mind and the body. There is a story told to us of two brothers. One of them had a spiritual bent of mind. He went to the *satsang* every day.

The younger brother preferred to go to the club in the evenings, and spent his time in gambling. When the young man was asked why he did not follow the example of his brother, he became angry. "Look, I am young," he retorted. "I should be out, making the most of my youth and enjoying myself. And not spend my precious leisure hours in singing *bhajans* and listening to discourses in the *satsang*. I need to build up my business, professional contacts!"

"Please brother," he would appeal, "I am asking you for a favour, just once, only once, come with me to the *satsang*!"

One fine day, the younger brother relented. He was in a good mood. "Just to please you, I will come with you to the *satsang*. But on one condition: after today, you must never, ever, mention the word '*satsang*' to me."

Next day, at a prior appointed time, the spiritually inclined brother went to pick up his brother from his house. But the young atheist had already left for the club, expressing his inability to join the brother for *satsang*.

This was repeated several times:

Today it was a business meeting; tomorrow, a party at the club and so on and so forth: as we all know, we don't have to try very hard to find excuses; they find us faster than we can think!

Do not postpone. Do not leave for tomorrow, what you can do today. Your stay on this earth plane is only for a limited period of time.

Begin your *sadhana* now, this very moment!

Here is a simple daily routine that I recommend to beginners:

1. Rise in the early hours of the dawn, when divine

vibrations are at their most positive.

2. Begin the day with a few minutes of silent prayer. Begin with five minutes, gradually increase the period to at least half an hour. If you persist in it, silence will become alive and the word of God will speak to you.

3. Take your first steps too, on the path of *abhyasa*. Start with a simple meditation exercise to still the wandering mind and give it focus and concentration. Mind is a monkey; it wanders from one object to another. When we are at work we do not realise the restlessness, the fickleness of the mind. But when we sit in silence – the mind begins to play its tricks, it wanders. For the beginners, love for God can be the greatest motivating, inspiring, uplifting factor. Therefore, begin your *abhyasa* by developing love for God.

4. Set aside some time during the day for meditation. You will make excellent progress on the path of *abhyasa*.

5. The life of meditation must be blended with the life of work. For we must not give up our worldly duties and obligations in order to meditate. We must return to our daily work, pouring into it the energy of the Spirit. Such work will bless the world.

6. Breathing is with you 24 hours a day. Use it to harness the power of concentration.

7. Shampoo your mind at least once a day! Shampooing means cleansing. The minds of so many of us are full of negative thoughts. We must cleanse them of their negativity.

8. Cultivate the subconscious mind: Always entertain positive thoughts. Truth is within! Wisdom is within! The source of all strength is within! Therefore, turn within!

WALK THE WAY OF TRUTH

We utter all kinds of lies, I doubt if any transaction of ours can ever be concluded without uttering one falsehood or the other. It is human nature to conceal one's own faults from one's own self. We are not able to face our own faults. When we are not true to our own self, how can we be true to others, how can we be true to our guru? God is Truth and if you want to go nearer to Him, then you should bear witness to the truth in deeds of daily life.

To travel the path of truth needs a tremendous amount of discipline, courage, steadfastness and determination. But the rewards of following this path are spectacular and what is more important, eternal.

How may we follow the practice of truth in everyday life? Let me offer a few practical suggestions:

1. Become aware of why you do not speak the truth: Is it out of fear? Or is it due to desire for gain? Address the root cause, and do not let negative emotions dictate your attitude. When you conquer them you learn to speak the truth in utter freedom.

2. Remember that the duty to speak the truth should not become a license to hurt another: therefore, practise truth along with kindness.

3. Do not rehearse half-truths or lies as excuses: if there has been a lapse on your part, admit the truth.

4. Learn the art of sincere apology. It involves being honest about yourself and being honest to the other person as well.

5. Not just outright lies, but also exaggerations and omissions amount to falsehood.
6. Remember that gossip, slander and rumour are some of the worst forms of falsehood.
7. Practise honesty in all your transactions, avoid malpractices in all business dealings.
8. Offering or accepting a bribe is also a form of dishonesty.

PRACTISE PURITY

This physical body is but a dwelling which we inhabit for a fleeting while. A time will come when we have to leave behind this physical form and move onward, forward.

Gurudev Sadhu Vaswani spoke of five aspects of our life, which needed purification: and, it applies to all of us, and not just aspiring *sadhakas* or seekers!

1. The very first is *Vaak* – voice, utterance, sound, speech which must be purified if you wish to grow in the perfect life.
2. *Prana* too must be purified, for it is our "life breath."
3. Next to *prana* is *Chakshu* which is interpreted as sight. If only we realised how many sins are committed due to untrained, uncontrolled sight!
4. Next comes *Shravan* – hearing. This too, must be purified. To listen to gossip, idle chatter, cruel criticism and malicious talk is to indulge in sin. Hear only the good, the pure, the wholesome and the true.
5. And finally comes *Bal or Shakti*, which means 'vital sense' or 'bodily vigour'. One of the saddest things in modern life is the lack of recognition of the sanctity of the vital

force, the creative force in us. One by one the senses must be disciplined, and thus prepared to walk the way of perfection.

SPIRITUALITY FOR BUSY PEOPLE

Do not make the mistake of assuming that spirituality is only for people who have nothing to do! In fact, 'busy' people perhaps need spirituality more than the rest of us, so that their 'busy'ness does not overwhelm their lives!

Practical Suggestion No.1

Always keep in mind the golden rule which states that you must do unto others, as you would have others do unto you.

Practical Suggestion No.2

Take care of your thoughts. Very often we pay scant attention to our thoughts. Thoughts lead to words and words to actions; and actions form our character.

Practical Suggestion No.3

Do not be in a hurry to give a promise. But if you have given a promise your life must bear witness to the ideal of truth. For truth is God.

Practical Suggestion No.4

Let prayer become a habit with you. Pray, pray and continue to pray. We forget that God acts at the right time. This applies not only to material requirements but, also, to mental and spiritual needs.

Practical Suggestion No.5

Accept whatever comes to you. Do not seek the 'pleasant': do not shun the 'unpleasant'. Rejoice in everything that happens. Meet every situation in life with the favourite prayer of St. Frances de

Sales: "Yes, Father! Yes, and always Yes!"

Practical Suggestion No.6

Whatever you do – do it wholly for the love of God. "Whatever you eat, whatever austerity you practice, whatever you give in charity, whatever you do, do it, O Arjuna, as an offering unto Me," says the Lord in the Gita. Can there be a simpler way of communing with God than this? This is the right way to practise the presence of God.

Practical Suggestion No.7

Remember death every day. We live in a world of uncertainty. There is only one thing of which we can be certain – that every passing day draws you closer to that moment when, leaving everything you hold dear and near behind – your wealth, friends, family, country – you will have to enter into the Great Beyond.

Gurudev Sadhu Vaswani said to us that we must not have any worry at all – except this one worry, that we have to set out on a long, endless journey but have made no preparations for the same.

Remembering death will also reinforce the fact that you are not the body you wear. The body is only a cage. It will drop down. The bird will fly away.

Practical Suggestion No.8

You must develop a good sense of humour. It helps you to meet the vicissitudes of life in your stride.

Practical Suggestion No.9

If you have wronged a person, then waste no time in setting right what has gone wrong. On the other hand; has someone wronged you? Forgive him, even before forgiveness is asked. And your mind will be at peace and the world around you will smile.

Practical Suggestion No.10

Spirituality is a gift of God: It cannot be earned. It cannot be acquired or possessed. For it is a reality given freely and spontaneously. All we can do is to keep the door of our heart open, and entreat God to enter therein. "When wilt Thou enter the home of my heart?" should be our constant prayer.

"Where is the dwelling of God?" asked the Rabbi of Kotzk of a number of learned men who visited him. They laughed at him and said: "What are you asking? God is Omnipresent. He is everywhere." The Rabbi then gave his answer and said: "God dwells wherever man lets Him in!"

May I, with folded hands, appeal to everyone of you, whose good fortune it is to aspire to walk the path of spirituality: "Let Him in! Let Him in! Let Him in!"

CONQUERING FEAR

WHAT IS FEAR?

Fear is the expectation of a clear and specific danger. It is natural to human beings in many situations. It teaches us to be cautious; it fosters our sense of self-preservation. It is what keeps us safe and secure.

Fear and anxiety are very similar; while fear is based on reality, or an exaggeration of a real danger, anxiety is based on an irrational or formless danger.

RECOGNISING FEAR

It would be true to say that fear permeates all aspects of our life on earth. Fear is not only present in us – it seems to exist in the very fabric of our institutions. It exists in families, workplace, schools, colleges, hospitals. The fear of failure, the fear of losing a match or a contest, is one of the worst kind of fears that haunts an individual. The stigma of failure makes us lose faith in ourselves. We are afraid of becoming unacceptable.

There are five basic types of fear identified by Dr. Forrest Church, eminent theologian and author:

1. Fright
2. Worry
3. Guilt
4. Insecurity
5. Dread

Human life is such that there will be times when we are overwhelmed by defeat, pain or suffering. These are the times to turn to someone – to find a shoulder to lean on.

WE ARE ALL VICTIMS OF FEAR

Fear casts its dark shadow over our lives at one time or another. The famous essayist, Montaigne, once confessed: "The thing I fear the most is fear." Fear is at the root of all our problems. Fear is the starting point for all evil. Fear gives rise to all our misfortune. It undermines our well-being. It robs us of happiness and destroys our peace of mind. It was Marie Curie who said: "Nothing in life is to be feared; it is only to be understood."

There are many people who live in a permanent state of anxiety. They will not be able to specify what they are afraid of. I often narrate the story of the businessman who refused to fly because his father was killed in a plane crash. I asked him how his mother had died. "She died peacefully, in her sleep," he replied. That had not stopped him from going to bed every day!

People feel lonely; people feel lost, people feel abandoned; they feel forsaken and forlorn. They have lost the sense of security which belongs to them as children of God; they have fallen into the abyss of fear! Fear is a poison that quickly circulates through the entire system, paralysing the will, producing queer, unpleasant sensations in the mind and the heart, and sometimes causing unhealthy conditions like ulcer, acidity and fainting.

FEAR CORRODES

The 'logic' of fear is truly illogical. We are afraid of losing our jobs – but we are afraid to go out and seek new positions. I know some people who are terrified of contracting a major illness – but they are even more scared to meet a specialist and go through a series of tests. Some young women are afraid of marriage, as they feel that they would lose their identity – but the idea of remaining single makes them feel insecure! There are very many old people who are terrified of the years that lie ahead of them – but they are haunted by the fear of death!

WHERE THE MIND IS WITHOUT FEAR

The *Bhagavad Gita* tells us:

> Meet the transient world
> With neither grasping nor fear,
> Trust the unfolding of life
> And you will attain true serenity...

Life demands of us that we live with courage. For those of us who live by our faith, as well as those who place their belief on science, life poses a series of unanswered – at times unanswerable – questions. Why do bad things happen to good people? Life is full of uncertainties, the unknown and the unknowable. Losing control, living with uncertainty generates fear – and this fear can be conquered by the right attitude – by love, kindness, faith and compassion. We must be unafraid to love – for love requires courage. I have always believed that the power of love is far greater than the power of hatred. If we are to confront the dark forces of destruction and annihilation, we must use the greatest weapon in our possession – the power of love.

It takes courage to love! Equally, it takes courage to forgive. There is suffering all around us. But wherever there is suffering, there are fearless, courageous, compassionate people who take on the sorrows of others as their own. They act without hesitation; they act selflessly; they care, they help, they heal!

FAITH GIVES YOU COURAGE

I was on board the S. S. Versova, travelling from Bombay to Karachi. Suddenly, a terrible storm arose at sea. I saw a little child – a boy who was barely six years old – sitting in a corner, calm, serene, undisturbed by the shrieking winds and the rolling waves.

I said to him gently, "It looks as if the steamer is about to sink – are you not afraid?" With a cherubic smile he answered, "What have I to fear when my mother is near?"

Our Mother – the Mother Divine is so near to each one of us. We have lost the childlike spirit. To be childlike is to rejoice in life, to love and laugh, to be free from care and anxiety.

This grace may be obtained through meditation, prayer and constant repetition of the Mother's name. Writing the name, again and again, is a great help.

Strike fear with the weapon of the spirit – the word of God. Utter the name that is dear to you – Krishna, Rama, Shyama, Jesus, Buddha, Allah, Nanak. Utter it again and again! Utter it in childlike faith and He whom you call will surely rush to your aid.

Very often, I repeat the following prayer from one of the songs composed by my Beloved Master, Sadhu Vaswani:

The sea is vast, my skiff is small:
I trust in Thee, who guard'st all!

The spoken word has the power to fight all evil – temptation, sin, anger and fear. This is why many people learn to recite a sacred *mantra* that is dear to them.

And in the measure in which our wills are blended with the Will of God, in that measure do we grow in strength, confidence and hope. Then it is that fear vanishes from our life, as mist before the morning sun. And we move through life trusting every ray of sunshine and every drop of rain, every rose and every thorn, every stone and every grain of sand, every river and every rock, trusting the sun and moon and stars, trusting thunder and storm, trusting everything and everyone!

FEARLESSNESS FOR THE ASPIRANT

Fearlessness is the first essential condition for spiritual growth.

Swami Vivekananda said "Be Fearless, Be Bold." Here are his words which I love to recall: "Stand up, be bold, be strong! Strength is life, weakness is death." Weakness is the one cause of suffering. We become miserable because we are weak. We lie, steal, kill and commit other crimes, because we are weak. We suffer, because we are weak. Where there is nothing to weaken us, there is no death, no sorrow.

Sadhu Vaswani said, "We are in the darkness of *avidya* – ignorance. We need to offer, again and again, the prayer of the ancient rishi – *Tamaso ma jyotir gamaya!* O Lord, out of darkness, lead me into light!"

CONQUER FEAR: PRACTICAL SUGGESTIONS

DON'T BE AFRAID

I recall the words of the great statesman, American President, Franklin D. Roosevelt, who delivered a memorable inaugural address on March 4, 1933 – at a time when America was facing the worst economic depression in her history. "Let me assert my firm belief that the only thing we have to fear is fear itself –

nameless, unreasoning terror which paralyses needed efforts to convert retreat into advance."

President Roosevelt proclaimed four basic freedoms –

Freedom of speech, Freedom of worship, Freedom from want and Freedom from fear.

The significant thing was that he included 'freedom from fear' as something essential and fundamental to human happiness. Being a victim of polio himself, unable to walk, he knew that fear could be more crippling than the disease itself.

A man who was travelling on a lonely road was robbed by bandits of all his possessions. They bound his hands and feet and dragged him into a forest. They blindfolded him and tied him to a rope and suspended him from a height.

"You are now hanging over the brink of a giddy precipice," they told him. "The moment you let go of this rope, you will be dashed to pieces on the rocks below." Terrified at the impending doom he gave in to despair, and he just let go of the rope, landing on the comforting solidity of mother earth! The grass was soft and moist to his touch. The earth smelt clean and refreshing. Quickly he untied his blindfold. The robbers had played a cruel trick on him and left him hanging just a few feet above the ground, so that they could make good their escape. When he let go, he was not letting go of his life, but only his fear!

Fort Alcan was a historical settlement of early European migrants in British Columbia, Canada. When Fort Alcan was abandoned after centuries as it had become old and decrepit, needy miners and other settlers in the area began to strip the place for anything valuable that they could lay their hands on – like lumber, electrical appliances, plumbing and hardware. While dismantling the jail in the settlement, they found mighty locks, reinforced steel doors, thick steel bars covering the windows and so on – but the walls of the prison were made of patented wallboard of clay and paper, merely painted to resemble iron. A good old push against the walls by a man built like a footballer – and the walls of the prison would have collapsed. But the amazing thing was that no one ever tried it – because no one thought it was possible! Alas, many of us are prisoners of fear, like the wretched inmates of Fort Alcan prison. We do not know our strength – and we do not realise that fear is nothing when we push against it and set it aside!

In the cold northern stretches of Europe, Canada and Russia, which are close to the Arctic Circle, temperatures fall far below 0° celsius in winter, and rivers and ponds freeze completely. You can find children ski and play on the frozen surfaces of these rivers and lakes, and people cross them walking, to get to the other side. On a dark, winter night, a man had to cross a wide frozen river. The people living on the riverbank assured him that it was perfectly safe to do so, since the river would stay frozen for weeks together.

The traveler decided to cross over, but he decided to crawl as slowly as he could, so that he could feel the ice and move cautiously. When he was near the middle of the frozen stream, he was startled by a sound in the distance, and caught sight of a tall and hefty man driving a team of four horses which were pulling a heavy load of pig iron. "Giddyap! Giddyap!" he urged the horses forward. The whole contraption sped across the surface of the river, as the man watched, crouching on all fours – and there was not the least sign of a crack in the ice. The man realised his folly in trying to crawl as he had done!

"Cowards die many deaths," goes the proverb. "The brave die but once." True it is that each of us has only one life – but how many of us die a thousand deaths in fear and nervousness!

An aircraft filled with passengers was flying across the Pacific when it hit turbulent weather. A business executive was flying long distance across the Pacific. A little boy travelling home for his holidays was seated next to him. The pilot sent signals to the passengers to fasten their seat belts, as the plane was about to run into stormy weather. Despite the enormous size of the plane and the power of its engines, the flight was jolted badly. The boy was scared and clung to the older man's arms. The man stroked the boy's head gently to reassure him. "Aren't you afraid?" whispered the boy, as the plane dipped suddenly. "No!" laughed the man. "This is real fun, isn't it? Aren't you enjoying yourself?"

An immediate change came over the little boy. His fear and tension left him and he too, began to enjoy the "fun", laughing and squealing delightedly as the plane dipped and swayed. The executive had taught the young one a valuable lesson in the art of living!

We are told that abstract thoughts (such as those which generate fear) arise from the higher brain centers; whereas the impulses that generate physical activity (such as walking, exercise and playing games) comes from the lower brain centers.

It seems to me that if we keep those lower centres of our brain busy by physical activity, the trouble caused by the higher centers would certainly abate in proportion! We would be better off expanding our physical energy in walking and other activities, rather than spending our mental energy in indulging useless fears!

Mary Ellen Chase tells us that manual labour is "not only good and decent for its own sake, but also for straightening out one's thoughts."

The best antidote for a confused head or of tangled emotions is to work with one's hands. Ironing clothes or scrubbing floors clears one's head.

A young man was victim to obsessive and recurrent fear. He

approached a psychiatrist to solve his problem. He advised the young man to jog every night till he was weary and tired – for this would ensure that he fell soundly asleep, thus effectively conquering his fears.

A stout heart and courageous spirit are vital if we are to live a life free from fear.

Fear destroys the soul, sapping our will to live.

The Persian poet Hafiz expresses this in memorable words when he tells us:

Fear is the cheapest room in the house.

I'd like to see you in better living conditions.

CULTIVATE THE WILL TO BE UNAFRAID

> It is His Will that I should cast
> My care on Him each day,
> He also bids me not to cast
> My confidence away.
> But oh! How foolishly I act
> When taken unaware,
> I cast away my confidence
> and carry all my care!

Freedom from fear is achieved through perseverance, tenacity and sheer will power.

Let me tell you the story of two frogs that fell into a bucket of cream. At first, they were bemused, but unafraid. Valiantly they tried their best to get out of the sticky fluid by climbing up the side of the slippery bucket. When they climbed eight inches, they slipped back ten inches. One of the frogs panicked. "We will never make it out of here alive," he sobbed. "I give up. I can't take it anymore." In his fear and frustration, he was drowned in the cream.

The other frog was resolute and determined. "I shan't be afraid," he told himself, "I shall find my way out. I shall live!" He went on and on, kicking with his back legs and climbing with his front legs. He fell back every time but did not give up his effort. Suddenly, he found that he hit something hard as he fell back on the cream. He turned to see what it was and discovered to his surprise that his kicking had churned up a sizable lump of butter! Quickly, he jumped on top of it and leaped out to safety!

Only they can conquer fear, who have willed themselves to do so!

Nirbhaya or fearlessness, has been the hallmark of the world's greatest intellects, martyrs and saints.

- This was how – Socrates drank hemlock, calmly and dispassionately.
- This was how – Christ allowed himself to be crucified.
- This was how – Mahatma Gandhi faced his assassin's bullets with the Name of the Lord on his lips.

These great souls had cultivated the will to be unafraid, the will to conquer fear at all costs!

A very wise man once wrote:

Let us not pray for easy lives. Let us pray that we may become stronger. Let us not pray for tasks equal to our powers. Let us pray for powers equal to our tasks.

"Onward, forward, Godward!" was the spiritual exhortation of my Master, Sadhu Vaswani. Real progress is only possible when we have the will power to pursue our chosen goals fearlessly.

Pat Boone was a popular singer who was resolute enough never to compromise his beliefs and values. He was offered thousands of dollars in those days to appear in three TV shows. He turned down the lucrative offers without second thoughts because these programs were sponsored by cigarette manufacturers and alcohol sellers. "I am personally opposed to both smoking and drinking," he said. "I do not want to influence anyone to take to these habits."

Pat Boone was unafraid of losing money, or indeed of his 'ratings' dropping. The thought of turning down lucrative contracts did not weaken his will power – he refused to compromise his ideals.

I am reminded of Hemingway's immortal words: "A man may be destroyed, but not defeated."

We must never underestimate mind power, the power of the will. Not only freedom from fear, but also our personal health, happiness and harmony, depends on thought habits. Truly has it been said that even happiness is the product of habitual right-thinking.

Mental sunshine is indeed very powerful! When you have the will to be free of fear, the sunshine of your faith and confidence will melt the ice of insecurity and dread. Mental sunshine will cause the flowers of peace and joy and serenity to bloom wherever you go! Therefore, cultivate the will to be unafraid – create your own mental sunshine!

There is a beautiful poem by an Elizabethan poet, Sir Edward Dyer, that talks about mind power:

> My mind to me a kingdom is,
> Such present joys therein I find,
> That it excels all other bliss
> That world affords or grows by kind.
> Though much I want which most would have
> Yet still my mind forbids to crave.

> I see how plenty suffers oft,
> And hasty climbers soon do fall;
> I see that those which are aloft
> Mishap doth threaten most of all;
> They get with toil, they keep with fear:
> Such cares my mind could never bear.

The poet tells us that the choice is always ours: to become greedy, avaricious, to toil, to become victims of mishap and live with fear – or else decide that our mind "could never bear" such behaviour. He knows that it is all in the mind. He makes up his mind that he would not fall prey to insecurity, fear and unhappiness. You can assert your will to create tranquillity and peace all around you.

Often, the worst fears come to us not from the outside, but from the mind within. By asserting your will power, by changing your mind, you can change your life and create tranquillity and peace all around you.

TO FEAR IS TO FORGET GOD

> Let nothing disturb thee;
> Nothing affright thee;
> All things are passing;
> God never changeth;
> Patient endurance
> Attaineth to all things;
> Who God possesseth
> In nothing is wanting;
> Alone God sufficeth!

"What is the meaning of life? What does it all mean? Why are we here? Where do we go from here?"

We are overwhelmed by such questions which bring down upon us a heavy load of doubts, fear and sorrow.

The first step in spiritual life is *Vishada*, the darkness of the soul. Even the first *adhyaya* (chapter) of The Gita is *Vishadha Yoga*. We must pass through darkness, so that the light can come!

Draupadi too, experienced this darkness of the soul when she cried out, "Everyone has abandoned me, all have left me – my kinsmen, my brothers, my father, my husbands – even You O, Krishna!"

Arjuna is a great warrior, a brave archer. He has come to the battlefield prepared to flight, confident of victory. He is Drona's greatest pupil; he is Sri Krishna's favourite disciple. But he is confounded by the grave situation that confronts him. In his weakness, Arjuna fails to listen to the voice within. The Lord knows that Arjuna's despair and pity are born of self-delusion – a form of *moha* or attachment. It is a major weakness and must be overcome by the man of true culture and religion. The blessed Lord tells Arjuna:

> Thy words sound wise, indeed, Arjuna!
> But thou art wasting grief where none is due.
> The truly wise in heart never grieve for those who
> live, nor yet for those who die!   (II, 11)

We may substitute 'fear' for grief in this context – for often, fear is also a form of delusion.

The story is told to us of a Frenchman, who incurred the displeasure of Napoleon and was put into a dungeon. His friends and family had forsaken him and forgotten his existence. In utter loneliness and despair, he took a stone lying in the corner of his cell and carved out the words, NOBODY CARES!

One day, a green shoot came up through the cracks on the damp and moist floor of the dungeon. Gradually, it began to grow and reach out upwards, toward the light in the tiny window at the top of the cell. The prisoner was given just adequate water to drink each day; he saved some of it and poured it on the blade of green, until it grew into a healthy plant with a beautiful blue flower. As the petals of the blue blossom opened, bending its head towards the light, the solitary prisoner crossed out the words previously written on the wall, and replaced them with the words: GOD CARES!

The Persian poet Saadi put it across boldly: "I fear God, and next to God I fear, most of all, him who fears Him not!"

Robert Ingersoll professed to be an atheist all his life. He heaped ridicule on God, religion, faith and believers. But when he was close to death, his soul was haunted by terror. In his fright, he is said to have cried out, "O God, if there be a God, have mercy on my soul, if I have a soul!" Caught in the clutches of the grim reaper, death, he seems to have realised that the greatest tragedy of life is to enter death without God, and go into an eternal Godless thereafter!

There is an amusing piece written by an anonymous writer to prove that even atheists cannot live without God:

"Religion is the opium of the people," said Karl Marx, the atheist. "Atheism is an integral part of Marxism," said Lenin. "Marxism is materialism. We must combat religion. This is the ABC of Marxism... Down with religion, long live atheism," said Lenin.

"Lenin is God," said Stalin.

Alas, we are ready to place our faith in wealth, power, strength and intellect. But the giver of all these is God – and if we cannot place our faith in Him, then our own lives are truly lost.

I recall how several years ago, something happened which threw me out of gear, and I fell into the slough of despondency. I was sad, dejected and depressed. I met my Beloved Master, Sadhu Vaswani. He looked at my wretched face but once; he did not look again. Nor did he speak to me a single word of comfort. He behaved as if he had not seen me. Living under the same roof, I was denied the privilege of seeing him, whom I loved deeply. The old man who resides within everyone, whispered to me: "Now you know how much he loves you!" It took me five days to understand that I must be of good cheer before I could be worthy of being admitted to Sadhu Vaswani's presence. Putting on a forced smile, I went up to him and asked for his blessings. He was loving as ever. As he enfolded me in a warm embrace, unbidden tears rolled down my cheeks. He spoke to me affectionately, as though nothing had happened. I understood what a blunder I had committed by appearing before him with a sullen face.

GOD MAKES ALL THINGS POSSIBLE!

> Doubt sees the obstacles
> Faith sees the way!
> Doubt sees the darkest night,
> Faith sees the day!
> Doubt dreads to take a step,
> Faith soars on high!
> Doubt questions, "Who believes?"
> Faith answers, "I"!

What is Faith?

Faith thaws out the fear which freezes the spirit, releases it, and sets it free – so the wise men tell us. I repeatedly tell my friends that fear is the child of unfaith. Fear and faith cannot exist together.

A woman was showing her valuable family heirlooms made of sterling silver to a visiting friend.

"How dreadfully tarnished they seem!" the friend exclaimed. "I cannot keep it bright unless I use it," said the woman. "That is just the way with faith," the friend replied. "You cannot keep your faith bright unless you use it!"

When fear knocks at the door of the heart, send your faith to open the door – and you will find there is no one there!

The great musician Handel passed through a severely trying time of life. His health was not good, his right side was paralysed which made him distraught. He gave in to hopelessness and deep despair. The future seemed to be a great big question mark.

With faith in God, he came out of the ordeal, and triumphed against all odds. This was when he composed his great piece of music in praise of the Lord – the famous *Hallelujah Chorus* which forms the grand climax of his immortal work, *Messiah*.

Have faith in God – He can! If we make this the mantra of our lives, we need never fear anything, ever in our lives! Repeat to yourselves again and again: I am not alone! God is with me! You will find that fear will not touch you.

God speaks to us in several ways to give us hope, courage and faith – if only we are sensitive enough to listen to Him!

There was a young widow who lived with her children in a small apartment in New York. Her husband had passed away recently, leaving her to fend for herself and three small children. He had left no savings and the family was plunged into poverty. It was the time of the great depression in America, and money and work were hard to come by. The young widow had great faith in the Lord, and she had instilled the same faith in her children. She said to them again and again, "Trust in the Lord! He will never forsake us!"

To earn her livelihood and support her children, she had rented a sewing machine, working at night with a dim light, sewing dresses and linen. She kept the home fires burning, as best as she could.

One of her customers had gone out of town, and her bill was pending. Now, she was up against a wall! She had to pay for the rental of her sewing machine – and the rent collector had warned her that the machine would be taken away if she did not pay the rent within 24 hours. There was a knock at the door – and the children trembled in fear.

"Mama, mama, what shall we do?" the children cried in fear. What could the mother do? What would become of them if the sewing machine was taken away?

"Hush my darlings!" the mother comforted them. The Lord is with us, and we have nothing to fear." She rose and opened the door. On the steps stood a stranger with a baby in his arms. He spoke with urgency. "Madam, I need your help very badly! You see, my wife has been admitted to hospital with an acute attack of appendicitis. There is no one at home to look after the baby. "We have just moved into this neighbourhood, and our landlord told us you are the right person to look after our baby, while my wife is in hospital. Please accept $50 as an advance from me. Will you please take care of the baby for us?" The woman stretched out her hands to receive the baby. "Go in peace, sir," she said to the stranger. "I shall take good care of the baby!"

When the stranger had left, the children crowded round her, laughing happily as the child gurgled and held out his little hand to them. "Wonderful are the ways of God," said the woman. "He never ever forsakes His children!"

Faith is deaf to doubts, dumb to discouragements and blind to impossibilities – for it knows nothing but success and optimism. It can lift its hands through threatening clouds and touch Him who can protect you from all harm and danger. Faith, I have heard, can make the uplook good, the outlook bright, the inlook favourable, and the future glorious!

Faith gives us a life-saving connection with God, in whatever circumstances we find ourselves. Faith is always on the shore, holding a rope out to us; when we take hold of it, we are sure to be hauled to safety. And when we have faith in God, it will reinforce our faith in fellow human beings and help us understand life and overcome our weaknesses.

LEARN TO RELAX AND DRIVE FEAR OUT!

"Fear comes from the heart. If ever you feel overcome by dread of some illness or accident, you should inhale and exhale deeply, slowly, and rhythmically several times, relaxing with each exhalation. This helps the circulation to become normal. If your heart is truly quiet you cannot feel fear at all," says Swami Paramahansa Yogananda.

Many people pass through life without ever realising that sense of peace and serenity which is what our elders had in mind, when they spoke about practising the presence of God.

Inner calm cannot be achieved by physical exertion. The word serenity is something that we only understand in the abstract, and not in practice. But serenity is a great gift that can be available to all of us when we are at one with the presence of God.

Imagine your mind to be the surface of a lake. When you are disturbed or agitated, the surface is whipped up by a furious storm. Huge waves arise, and lash against the shore in a fury. It is a frightening display of the violent force of wind and water. And then, the wind abates, and the waves gradually subside. The lake's surface becomes still and smooth as a mirror.

This lake is our mind. We can calm the spirit, when the fury of our thoughts and anxieties are quietened down. It is in such stillness that we achieve strength and peace of mind. It is then that our fears are vanquished, and we achieve joy and serenity.

God is perfect. God is the source of all that is best in our lives.

Helpful, healing, wholesome thoughts come to us during periods of stillness, prayer and meditation.

Fear often leads to extreme nervous tension. When our minds are haunted by fear, the waters of the soul are muddied. We need to retreat, so that the soul may be refreshed. If the soul is to be cleansed, we need to take a dip in the waters of silence – for silence is a great healer. It is only in a serene, tranquil state of mind that we can feel the healing power of God flowing into us.

Through practice, we can, at will, enter this realm and contact God. When we do so, we become conscious of infinite power, a wondrous peace, and a beautiful sense of serenity within.

The first step to this inner serenity is relaxation.

So many diseases of the present day – heart attacks, high blood pressure, nervous breakdown, migraine, asthma – are due to this built-up tension.

There are several methods of relaxation, and you can follow one that suits you best. Here is a simple, easy, eleven step method that I recommend:

1. Lie on your back on the floor – or sit on the floor in a *sukhasana* (comfortable posture). You may, if you like, sit on a chair with your feet gently touching the floor. Begin by taking a few deep breaths, exhaling very slowly, so that the lungs are completely emptied out.

2. Imagine yourself in the loving, immediate and personal presence of the Lord. Picture yourself sitting at His Lotus Feet, with your arms girdling His ankles, your head resting at His feet. Say to yourself, "Here is true rest. Here is peace. Here is relaxation. In Thy presence, Lord, my fears and frustrations, worries and anxieties, depressions and disappointments, tensions and tribulations vanish as mist before the rising sun. I feel at peace… I am relaxed…"

3. At this point, you begin to relax each part of your body, consciously. To relax a muscle, you must first tighten it, then let it go. As you let it go, it may perhaps help you to utter the magic words, "Let go, let go, let God…"

4. Turn your attention to the muscles around the eyes. Relax – relax – relax. Open the eyes and imagine that the eyelids have become heavy. Let them drop on the eyes. Lift them and shut them three times.

5. Move on to the muscles around the mouth. Tighten them and let go. Relax – relax – relax.

6. Relax your facial muscles. Clench your teeth, then relax, letting your face go limp. Relax – relax – relax.

7. Repeat the process throughout the body: neck, right shoulder, elbow, forearm, wrist, hand, fingers, left shoulder,

elbow, forearm, wrist, hand, fingers – back, chest, abdomen, buttocks, calves, ankles, feet, toes. Push your toes down on the floor, stretch and relax. Pull your feet up towards the legs, stretch and relax. Relax – relax – relax.

8. Breathe in deeply; stretch your whole body; relax and exhale. Repeat this three times. Relax – relax – relax. Tell yourself that you are now relaxed, calm, serene, peaceful. Reinforce the picture of yourself resting joyfully at the Lotus Feet of the Lord – calm, relaxed, serene, peaceful.

9. You are now lighter than air, moving upwards, upwards, floating as a cloud – calm, relaxed, peaceful, serene.

10. You are in the presence of the Lord. Offer this simple prayer to Him: "Thou art by me, a living and radiant presence, and I am relaxed, calm, peaceful, serene." Repeat this prayer a few times. You are now completely relaxed.

11. When you wish to close this exercise in relaxation, rub the palms of your hands together, place them gently on the eyelids, and gently open the eyes.

To enter into the Peace of God is to relax and stand still – wherever you are!

DON'T BE AFRAID OF THE FUTURE

When should we worry?
When we see the lilies of the field
Spinning in distress,
Taking thought to manufacture
All their loveliness;
When we see the little birds

Building barns for their store –
Then't will be time for us to worry –
But not before!

There are many people I know who live in constant fear of what the future holds for them. They anticipate nothing but trouble, and fear of the future has become part of their mental make-up. They live in constant insecurity, and in doing so, they lose much of the joy of living. "What if the stock exchange crashes?" "What if I should meet with an accident?" "What if my child were to fall ill…" And so on and so forth their mind wanders, from fear to fear.

I tell people again and again: you should not make yourself miserable, by thinking of the past or of the future. The past is a cancelled cheque. The future is just a promissory note. The present is the only cash in hand – so use it wisely and well. Make the most of the here and the now!

How many of us break our backs to provide against dangers that never come! How many people struggle to lay up riches which they never enjoy; to provide for exigencies that never happen; to prevent troubles that never come; and they sacrifice present comfort and enjoyment in guarding against the wants of a period they never live to see!

You must learn to live in the present! Give your best to the present! Concentrate on the task you are doing. Let all your energy and attention be focused on the present moment.

An old lady once remarked to a friend, "I keep worrying about the future constantly. I can't tell you how afraid I am at times!"

The friend urged her to cast her fears and worries at the Lord's Feet and live a life free from fear.

"Oh, but I can't do that!" exclaimed the lady. "If I don't worry, I begin to feel very bad!"

How sad it is that we should punish ourselves thus! Truly has it been said, "A day of worry is more exhausting than a day of work." Honest work seldom hurts us. Nobody has been known to have been killed by hard work. But fear, stress and worry can be fatal.

A French soldier in World War I, carried with him this little message as an antidote for fear:

Of two things, one is certain. Either you are at the front or behind the lines. If you are at the front, of two things one is certain. Either you are exposed to danger, or you are in a safe place. If you are exposed to danger, of two things one is certain. Either you are wounded, or you are not wounded. If you are wounded, of two things one is certain. Either you recover, or you die. If you recover, there is no need to be afraid. If you die, you can't be afraid any more. So why be afraid?

In the voyage of our life, we must learn to bring down the shutters that keep out the past with all its errors and failures. Equally, we must also shut out the unborn future, so that we may live in the present. When we close the doors that shut out the past and the future, we will find that the ship of life sails smoothly ahead!

Should we constantly burden our hearts and souls with tomorrow's problems and tomorrow's responsibilities? Can we not walk with God today and trust Him for the morrow?

Here is the text I found on a New Year card sent to me:

I said to the man at the gate of the year, "Give me a light so that I may tread safely into the unknown. He replied, "Go out into the darkness and put your hand into the hand of God. That shall be to you better than light and safer than a known way."

So, let me repeat to you: Walk with God today and trust Him

for the morrow!

LOVE LEAVES NO ROOM FOR FEAR

Wealth does not count; words do not count; actions count! Selfless deeds of kindness and compassion count most of all!

Mr. and Mrs. Kapoor lived on the top floor of a high-rise building overlooking the sea, in an exclusive suburb of Mumbai. For several years after they moved into their apartment, the other flat on their floor remained vacant. The Kapoors were very happy, they had exclusive use of the common terrace. They lined the corridors and landing with their potted plants.

Nearly ten years after they came to live there, the neighbours returned. Mr. and Mrs. Kapoor were not pleased. They peeped through the little watch-hole set on their door and frowned as their new neighbors settled in. Soon thereafter, the doorbell rang. Mr. Kapoor, who had been peeping through the watch-hole tiptoed back into the living room and said to his wife, "They are here! The lady is carrying a bowl." "What a nuisance!" sighed Mrs. Kapoor. "I dare say she has come to borrow sugar or tea, or some such thing."

"Don't encourage that kind of thing!" hissed Mr. Kapoor. "Turn them away immediately. Otherwise they will start knocking at our door for every least reason."

"Don't you worry my dear," said Mrs. Kapoor firmly. "I shall show the lady her place." With her lips firmly pursed and a hostile frown on her brows she walked up to the door and opened it unsmilingly. "Good Morning!" greeted the couple at the door. The lady held out a crystal dish filled with delicious *mithai* and dry fruits. "We are your new neighbors and we have brought you a little *prasad* after our house-warming *pooja*!"

With a little gesture of friendship, the neighbors had conquered the hostility and selfishness of the Kapoors.

"Charity begins at home," we have often heard. Yes, indeed, charity may begin at home, but it would indeed be a pity if it stays there! I therefore urge you, in the unforgettable words of my Master, Sadhu Vaswani: Give! Give! Give! Give not only to those you love – but also to those who do not love you. Give especially to the unfortunate and the deprived – give to those whom you don't want to give! You will receive much from your giving – you can achieve freedom from fear!

GATEWAYS TO HEAVEN

LIFE IS A GATEWAY TO ETERNITY

Let's start with a beautiful prayer in the words of my Gurudev, Sadhu Vaswani:

> Far away from you, I have wandered.
> Show me the way, shower Your Grace on me.
> Wherever I am, wherever I may be, whatever I may do,
> In every thought, in every word, keep me close to Your heart!

A wanderer can never be happy. A vagabond can never experience stillness.

Many people say that this material world of ours is a prison, and the only thing to do here is to escape as best we can. But, let me say to you, this world is what you make of it. Do not forget for a moment, that it is through this human birth that you can attain freedom. Each one of us has been given the golden opportunity of the human birth, which is, in itself, a gateway to freedom, emancipation and liberation. It is for us to choose between making this a prison, or a gateway to liberation.

Are we not, all of us, vagabonds and wanderers?

What is the root cause of this wandering?

Birth after birth have we wandered. Lifetime after lifetime, have we inhabited this world of illusion, as vagabonds from one incarnation to another. And the wandering still continues.

That is because of our alienation from God, separateness from the source of all life, from God, the Creator of this universe.

When you look for happiness, you are not likely to find it. You recognise then that true happiness is in self-realisation. When you accept the Will of God, in every circumstance, in every situation, during every crisis, every trauma, it will unlock for you the gateway to God's kingdom; it will also lead you to the bliss and peace of heaven on earth.

The spiritual path is not easy and smooth! There are many obstacles on the way. Even when you have scaled the heights, there is ever present, a danger of falling off the peak. To remain safe and secure in spiritual attainment, one needs the protection of the Guru or the grace of God.

If we cultivate this spirit of acceptance, that whatever He wills can only be good for me, we will discover the peace that surpasses understanding, and the joy that knows no ending!

How may we make the most of this life – the gateway that can lead us to the Kingdom of God?

Let me offer you a few practical suggestions:

1. Fill your heart with love – love for God, love for your fellow men, birds and animals, nature, and of course, yourself!

2. In everything that you do, pour out the best that is in you. Make your entire life – an offering at the Lotus Feet of the Lord.

3. Let go, let go, let God! Let go of everything. Let God take charge of your life and affairs. Letting go permits divine ideas to flow, divine power to work, divine order to bless your body, mind, soul and your activities.

4. Never think or talk negatively.

5. See the good in everyone. Be blind to the faults of others. Constant complaining and criticising only corrodes your spirit.

6. Do not allow circumstances and your own desires to master you. Rather, aim to be a master over circumstances and your own animal appetites and desires.

Life can be changed; life must be changed for the better. Just think of joy, peace, purity, love, perfection and prosperity. You will find that you need not take the trouble to go to heaven; your life upon earth will become a heaven for you and those around you!

Happiness belongs to those who are immersed in the faith that God can never fail us. In all that happens to us, there is a meaning of His Mercy. The Great Universe has a perfect scheme of things and whatever happens, has a meaning and a purpose. We should accept the divine will, and look upon all that happens to us as *prasad* from God! Such an attitude can be cultivated by praying to God. In the words of Sadhu Vaswani:

> Keep me close to your heart,
> Let me not wander,
> In joy and in sorrow,
> Thy Will, not mine, be done!

WHAT IS HEAVEN?

There are as many different concepts of heaven as there are different religious faiths.

To the Chinese, heaven is a place where ancestors reside.

In the Gospel according to Matthew, we read: "Again, the kingdom of heaven is like unto treasure hid in a field; which when a man hath found, he hideth, and for joy thereof, goeth and selleth all that he hath, and buyeth that field." (Matthew 13:44)

Luke offers a subtler definition: "The Kingdom of God does not come visibly, nor will people say, 'Here it is' or 'There it is' because the Kingdom of God is within you." (Luke: 17:20-21)

In Islam, the state of blessed after life is referred to as paradise; according to the Holy Quran, paradise is a beautiful garden, where the chosen few will reside in eternal bliss.

According to Roman Catholic belief, heaven is the realm of the blessed trinity of father, son and holy spirit, as also the home of the blessed Virgin Mary, who is known as the queen of heaven; it is a place where the angels and the saints reside. In this heaven, the soul rests perfectly in God, and does not, or cannot desire anything else than God.

In the Protestant faith, true believers get to spend eternity with God, and with other good souls like themselves. It is a place of great joy, without any of the negative aspects of earthly life.

Zoroastrianism offers us an interesting perspective, because, unlike many other religions, it claims that everyone will eventually get into heaven, though it might take a while. The paradise of Zoroastrianism is attained by crossing the Bridge of the Separator, which widens when the righteous approach it.

For Hindus, *moksha* is the highest goal. It means liberation and release from the world of *samsara,* the eternal cycle of birth, suffering, death, and rebirth. It is a state of union with God.

There are quite a few gateways that can lead us on to this beautiful state of Liberation.

We all have a free, fair and equal chance of making it across those sought-after gates.

FIRST GATEWAY:
FAVOUR FAITH

In love we know that we belong to Him who takes care of us as a mother takes care of her only child. Such faith is not just reassuring and comforting: it brings about miracles in your daily life.

Someone asked me: "What makes your life beautiful?"

I said: "I have a Friend." Yes, He protects me. He guards me in illness. He blesses me every day. And He stretches forth His arms of love to enfold me in silence and darkness of the night. He is your Friend, too. Indeed, He is the Friend of friends. And may your faith in Him shine and shine and make your crowded life truly divine!

— Sadhu Vaswani

He who has faith, has everything. If you wish to grow in faith, then pray for faith as a famished person prays for food and a thirsty person for water.

What is it to have faith? It is nothing but to accept God's plan for you – to surrender to the Will Divine. It is to feel sure that whatever God does is always for the best.

Sri Ramakrishna, speaking to his disciples, said again and again, "The man of faith is like a python. He moves not in search of food; his food comes to him."

Faith belongs to those of us who have learnt to love. For in love, we renounce our 'ego', and rise above the cares and worries of earthly existence.

A pious lady was talking to her little nephew about the efficacy of prayer. Suddenly, the little boy asked, "If I ask God to help me find my marbles, will He answer my prayer?" The lady assured him that God would indeed do so.

"May I kneel down and pray to God now?" the boy asked.

His aunt having given her consent, the little boy knelt by his chair, closed his eyes and prayed silently. Then he rose, and went about his work contentedly.

Next day, the lady asked him if he had found his marbles. She hoped that his simple faith would not be tested adversely.

"No aunt, I haven't found them," the boy replied. "But God has made me not want to find them!"

God does not always answer our prayers in the way we wish or expect, but if we are sincere, He will take from us the desire for what is contrary to His Will!

Faith is not just a solution to all our problems – it is a transformation of our inner existence; it helps us cultivate hope and optimism, which have the power to change our attitude, change our pattern of thinking, and thus change our lives for the better!

My Master, Sadhu Vaswani, often said to us, "God upsets our plans to set up His own. And His plans are always perfect. In His divine wisdom He knows what is not good for us, and He will not grant it to us."

We complain that our prayers have not been answered. This is not true. EVERY PRAYER IS ANSWERED. The trouble with us is, we fail to recognise the answer.

God answers our prayer in four ways:

The first is "Yes." We ask for something; we pray to God, and He says, "Yes, my child. Here it is; I give you what you asked for."

The second is "No." For a good reason, God tells us, "No, my child, I will not grant your prayer."

The third is "Wait." It is as if God tells us that the time is not ripe for us to receive what we want. So He tells us, "Wait. The time is not yet come."

The fourth is, "Here is something better." We have asked for one thing, but He grants us something else and says, "Here is something different, something better that I want to give you."

When the answer is in the affirmative, when God says "Yes,"

we feel very happy. We thank Him; and our faith in Him becomes stronger.

But the other three answers – "No", "Wait" and "Here is something better" – it is these three that test our faith.

God loves us. He has a plan for each one of us; and His plans are perfect. If what we ask in prayer goes contrary to God's plan, that prayer is not granted – for sure, this is for our own good.

We need to believe that He is there with us, working through us, to perform His miracles. We may not see how He works, but He is sure to help us out of our suffering. It is this profound truth that is expressed in the words of the Lord in the Gita:

Know this for certainty, Arjuna: My devotee is never lost.

All we have to do is cling to Him in faith and hope: He will not, indeed He cannot let us down!

Believe that with God, all things are possible! Many doctors have assured us that they have seen men, after all therapy had failed, lifted out of affliction and disease by the serene effect of faith. Faith seems to overcome even the so-called 'laws of nature'. And the occasions on which prayer has dramatically done this have been termed 'miracles'.

Just by asking for His help, our deficiencies are set right and we are restored, rejuvenated and strengthened.

Henry Ford made a statement, "I believe God is managing our affairs and that He doesn't need any advice from me. With God in charge, I believe everything will work out for the best in the end. So what is there to worry about?"

Here are some aids to cultivate such faith:

1. The first essential thing is a change of outlook. We depend

too much on ourselves, our efforts and endeavors. We keep God out of the picture. But we need to understand that above all efforts is HIS WILL. So let not our work be egotistic – but dedicated as an offering to him.

2. The second essential thing is to share what we have with others. This is one of the laws of life – the more we give, the more we get out of the little that remains.

3. Do not be frightened of anything. Trust in the Lord and face the battle of life.

4. Trust in Him. Turn to Him for everything you need.

5. We must contact God again and again. It is necessary for us to repeat His Name again and again to pray without ceasing. A prayer which may prove helpful is, "Lord! Make me a channel of Thy Mercy!"

6. To become a channel of His mercy, we must surrender all we are and all we have, at His Lotus Feet. So may we become His instruments of help and healing in this world of suffering and pain. All our cares and burdens are borne by the Lord Himself.

The life of faith is a blessed, carefree life. To be truly free is to be born anew, to become a pure child of God.

SECOND GATEWAY:
PRACTISE PATIENCE

There are many virtues which can be cultivated by means of other virtues: thus, love leads you on to compassion; compassion directs you on to selflessness and service of the suffering ones; faith gives you hope; truth guides you to honesty and integrity. But you need a lot of fortitude to learn the wonderful virtue of patience!

The Dictionary defines patience as: the quality of being patient, as in the bearing of provocation, annoyance, misfortune, or pain, without complaint, loss of temper, irritation, or the like.

Patience is used to refer to quiet, steady perseverance; even-tempered care; and also diligence: we praise people who work with patience. Patience is not just a virtue; it is a compendium of several good qualities.

A beautiful prayer goes thus: "God, give me the power to change the things I can, accept the things that I cannot change, and the wisdom to know the difference." Sadly, we spend much of our time and energy trying to control things which we cannot control. This futile effort leaves us frustrated, impatient and embittered. We need to develop the virtues of patience and acceptance – not as passive, helpless victims, but as wise and understanding human beings.

Tolerance, understanding, acceptance: the world has great need of these today. Most importantly, we need to be patient with ourselves! Patience is essential for everyone who wishes to make progress on the spiritual path. In this, as in many other things, Nature is our best teacher. If we observe Mother Nature, we will perceive that nature is never in haste. Take the sun, it religiously rises in the morning and sets in the evening, giving its light to the earth and sustaining all the creatures on it. Likewise, the trees stand firm in sunshine and rain. They do not complain, in fact they bless us by providing us with shade, fuel, wood and fruit. The true seeker learns to cultivate endurance, compassion and selflessness from the earth.

In today's world of haste and waste, stress and tension, trials and tribulations, patience assumes a great worth. Patience is necessary to avoid dissipating our energies.

Patience is the alchemist who turns every blow into a blessing, every burden into a benediction. As the pilgrim moves on the path, he is tried and tested, as gold is tested by being thrown into the crucible.

The man of patience thrives on suffering: the more he suffers, the more his soul shines. The great *Sufi* teacher and mystic, Rumi, unfolds a very beautiful picture in his *Masnavi*. He writes, "There is an animal called the porcupine. It is made stout and big by blows of the stick. The more you cudgel it, the more it thrives. The soul of a true believer is, verily, a porcupine. The more it is chastised, the more it thrives. So it is that God's chosen ones have to bear a greater share of suffering than other worldly men. Suffering gives strength to their souls."

There are situations in everyday life that tax our patience; acquiring a license or special permission from a government department; or being stuck in a traffic jam; life seems excessively stressful!

Impatience is one of the worst barriers to listening. We must cultivate patience and courtesy, at least to the extent of allowing the speaker to finish whatever he has to say.

"Patience is bitter, but its fruit is sweet," said Rousseau. Anger is the killer of patience.

I often tell my friends that the greatest famine in the world today is the famine of understanding; no two people seem to be able to understand each other. Only the spirit of understanding and patience can foster good human relationships:

1. Avoid doing things in haste. Make a list of tasks to be completed, and go about each one systematically, taking the help of others if available.
2. Change your attitude to life and people, so that you may overcome stress and irritation.
3. In this as in other things, acceptance is crucial to peace and

harmony. Accept that there are some things in your life which are not under your control, and that you cannot change everything and everyone around you to suit your way of functioning.

4. Learn to relax consciously in stressful situations. Deep breathing is an instant de-stressor, and in the long run, meditation also helps you to become stable, calm and patient.
5. When a situation becomes impossible for you to handle, learn to let go. Let go, let go, let God.
6. Remember, good things always come to people who wait, but very few good things in life come immediately!
7. Learn to take a break. Discover at least twice a week the joy of doing nothing – absolutely NO thing!
8. Get your priorities right. Ultimately, peace and good will are far more important than instant gratification of your desires. Be kind, tolerant, patient and understanding.

THIRD GATEWAY:
SAVOUR *SATSANG*

Man's life is so crowded with mundane activities, that he rarely has time for self-study and introspection. He seldom finds himself in that expansive, tranquil mood of silence and reflection, where he can listen to God, and chant the Name Divine in the heart within.

Our worldly desires are like the salty waters of the sea. Such waters can never quench man's thirst.

Work is essential for a human being. It disciplines his mind and exercises his body. Work is a great boon. But we must remember, work is a means, it is not an end. Livelihood must never be confused with life. Hence, even while you are attending to your work, stay connected to the Source of all Life; stay in constant touch with God. Set aside personal time, spend some of that valuable time in any form of *sadhana* that appeals to you. If you give eight or nine hours a day to your work, it should not be difficult to spare one or two hours to your spiritual growth! This will help you achieve the kind of inner peace and bliss that work can never bring to you.

Have you ever wondered what is the noblest thing on the earth? Let me answer, in the words of my Gurudev, "The noblest work is to cultivate the soul." To cultivate the soul, we should sow the seeds of love, selfless service and devotion. We should chant the Name Divine, set apart time for silent communion with God, and offer the service of love to those who are less fortunate than we are. We will then experience divinity in our everyday life. The *satsang* offers all this and more to you, in one beautiful package deal!

Naam Smaran is not mere chanting, it is a yearning.

Very often in the *satsang*, I open my eyes after a meditation or a prayer, and I get the feeling that some of the *satsangis* are present there only physically. Their thoughts wander. If they would sit in quietude and focus on the *naam kirtan*, they could experience many mystical insights. Their physical ailments would disappear. They would taste a rare peace that is born of true inner bliss.

When a man falls ill he goes to the hospital to be treated. *Satsang* is like the hospital, which will treat the disease called 'evil'.

Who is a true *satsangi*? Not the one who attends the *satsang*, but the one who absorbs the pure vibrations of the *satsang*, listens to every word carefully, goes home and ponders over the teachings and puts them into practice. Some of these devotees will surely reap the benefits of the pure and sacred environment, while the others will make a beginning in the right direction.

Satsang creates pure and positive vibrations which neutralise the negative emotions of man. When we go to *satsang*, we get to hear discourses of holy men, participate in the recitation of sacred scriptures and singing of soulful *bhajans*. All of this helps to raise the levels of positive vibrations and energises us. For a short time at least, we forget our mundane worries and get immersed in the pure waters of the Spirit.

Unfortunately for us, these emotions of sublimity do not last long. The moment we leave the *satsang*, we are submerged in worldly concerns.

What is the reason? Why is our spiritual effort so short lived?

That is because the mind is not used to *abhyasa*. If we could sit in quietude and focus on the *naam kirtan*, we would experience many mystical insights. Our physical ailments would disappear. We would taste a rare peace that is born of true inner bliss.

FOURTH GATEWAY:
TIE YOURSELF TO TRUTH

There is no religion higher than truth. Such is the respect we accord to *satya*, that the motto of the Government of India, the inscription on the seal of the state and the national emblem records this great statement from the Vedas. *Satyameva Jayate*... Truth Alone Triumphs.

The leader of a certain sect., once challenged Guru Nanak thus: "You talk of God as if you know Him. Can you show us where He dwells? And can you tell us what is His name?"

Guru Nanak's answer was simple and straight from the heart:

"He is the One Abiding Reality in this ever-changing world. And His name is *sat* – he is the Truth of all Truths."

This, the fundamental belief of Sikhism, is enshrined in the opening invocation of the prayer at the Gurudwara: *Ek Onkaar... Satnaam...*

Truth is the very first step that the seeker has to take on the path to salvation. Truth is dear to God, and dear to men of God. It is every guru's dearly held wish that his disciples should always bear witness to the truth in their daily life, and that they should always refrain from falsehood.

We will face great difficulties in our quest for Truth; but the man of divine qualities overcomes them by his perseverance on the path. Many of us give up the effort. "It is an impossible ideal to put into practice," we assert. "It is not just unattainable; it is impractical," we lament.

We also have the much revered concept of *Satyam, Shivam, Sundaram* – the embodiment of truth, goodness and beauty that is Lord Shiva. The ten *yamas* or restraints recommended by the ancient scriptures, urge the seeker to refrain from falsehood.

Our Vedas urge us not merely to speak the truth, but also to speak only that truth which is pleasant, useful and is not hurtful to others.

The path of truth is not for the weak-willed and cowardly: as Emerson once put it, "God offers to every mind its choice between truth and repose. Take which you please – you can never have both." To travel the path of truth one needs a tremendous amount of discipline, courage, steadfastness and determination. But the rewards of following this path are spectacular and most important, eternal.

How may we follow the practice of truth in everyday life? Let me offer a few practical suggestions:

1. Become aware of why you do not speak the truth: Address the root cause, and do not let negative emotions like fear

and greed and ill-will dictate your attitude. Practise truth along with kindness without hurting another.

2. Speak the truth at the appropriate time: not when your listeners are not prepared to take them.
3. Do not rehearse half-truths or lies as excuses to utter to friends: admit the truth.
4. Learn the art of sincere apology. Learning to say sorry is one of the most difficult acts of truth.
5. Not just outright lies, but also exaggerations and omissions amount to falsehood: speak the truth, the whole truth and nothing but the truth.
6. Remember that gossip, slander and rumour are some of the worst forms of falsehood.
7. Hypocrisy and pretence are also akin to falsehood.
8. Practise honesty in all your transactions, especially when they relate to money matters.
9. Offering or accepting a bribe is also a form of dishonesty.

To follow the path of truth – live a simple life.

FIFTH GATEWAY: EMBRACE COMPASSION

Compassion is the crown of all virtues. It is closely linked to all the cardinal virtues. It arises out of love and charity and is the basis of *seva* or service. My Master, Sadhu Vaswani, who was a Messiah of compassion, put it in admirable words: "Service of the poor is worship of God." Hindus believe that the Divine is manifested in every living being. This leads to the ideal of reverence for all life, and its corollary, *daya* or compassion, and *ahimsa* or non-violence.

All major religions of the world lay emphasis on compassion – compassion in thought, word and action!

Buddha taught that human beings are afflicted with various kinds of *dukha* or sufferings, associated with old age, sickness, death, grief, pain and despair – this requires the spirit of compassion to wipe out human suffering.

Christianity, too, regards compassion as a blessed quality. "Blessed are the merciful," Jesus said. "For they shall obtain mercy."

Islamic scholars tell us that compassion is central to Islam – in fact, it represents the true spirit of Islam. The names *Rahman* and *Rahim* (The compassionate, the merciful) are the names by which every devout muslim invokes allah in his daily prayers.

A Jewish teacher tells us:

"Kindness gives to another. Compassion knows no other."

The greatest form of compassion can only come by understanding the central concept of *Vedanta:* that the life that sleeps in stones and minerals, the life that stirs in plants and trees, the life that dreams in animals and birds is the same life that awakes and breathes in man. And this life is the very spark of the Life Universal.

Compassion without wisdom is ineffective; wisdom without compassion is soulless. When a compassionate heart is linked to an insightful mind, then we can make a significant contribution to peace upon this earth.

Once Gandhiji and Kasturba were visiting a village. While Gandhiji was busy talking to the men, Kasturba went among the women and spoke to them of cleanliness and personal hygiene. "You must bathe every day," she told them earnestly, "and change into clean, washed clothes."

A poor woman took *Ba* into her hut and said to her, "*Ba*, the only clothes I have are these which I'm wearing now. How can I change clothes and wash them daily?"

Ba was profoundly moved by the woman's plight. She spoke of the incident to Gandhiji later that day.

"What can we do for them?" she asked him in anguish.

During those days Gandhiji used to wear the traditional Indian clothes: *dhoti, kurta, angavastra* and turban. Forthwith he decided that he would wear only a loincloth for so many of his brothers and sisters had no clothes on their backs!

Gurudev Sadhu Vaswani too had such an awareness, compassion and sensitivity as a child. Sometimes, as he sat down to his meals and heard the cry of a passing beggar, he would take away his food to share it with the hungry one. From the beginning of his days, he was filled with the spirit of compassion for all who were in suffering and pain.

When we give of ourselves, of our time and our wealth, we must learn to give in the right spirit, the spirit of true compassion, for "The gift without the giver is bare," as the saying goes.

All that we give in love and compassion, we give to the Lord Himself. The first beneficiary of such service is not the receiver, but the giver – for it takes him closer to the Lord.

To understand how we can walk the way of true compassion, here are a few practical suggestions:

Compassion begins in awareness. The first step on the path of compassion is to be aware that the One Life flows in all.

The second step of compassion is the acknowledgement that all Creation is One family; all the people of the world, even birds and animals are our younger brothers and sisters in the One family of Creation.

Compassion begins in awareness; but it is not enough to feel compassion, or express compassion through speech. Compassion should be expressed in action, in deeds of daily life, in little acts of kindness and love.

Selective compassion is selfish compassion! True compassion knows no barriers of caste, creed, race or faith. It falls like the gentle rain on all humanity, all of creation.

Compassion is not giving of your money and your assets: true compassion is giving your love, giving yourself in an endless stream of sympathy that flows out to all.

Compassion is a divine attribute, and takes you closer to God. Therefore, compassion should be non-judgmental, and offered freely. It is the spark of compassion which binds us to our fellow human beings and takes us closer to God Himself.

God is all Love. God is all Wisdom. He expects us to live and work not merely for our own pleasure and our own benefit, but also for the service and benefit of others. Is it not more blessed to give than to receive?

Compassion does not require a hefty wallet, strong limbs or heroic deeds or great and austere sacrifices. A helping hand, a friendly word or gesture, a kind smile will more than suffice! And let me add, in the words of Mark Twain: "Kindness is a language which the deaf can hear and the blind can read!"

Compassion is the very root of religion, even as pride is the root of sin; let us be kind, let us practise compassion till the very last breath of our being.

SIXTH GATEWAY: HUMILITY HELPS

Sant Kabir says:

> Speak sweetly,
>
> Walk humbly,
>
> Let your hands never be tired of giving.
>
> Then why need you to the forest go,
>
> The Lord is with you already!

There is no need for you to go in quest of God. For God, the source of joy and happiness will come in quest of you – and meet you.

The truly humble are the truly happy. And what we need to be truly happy is not a change in outer circumstances, but deliverance from slavery to the self, the petty ego. This ego sits as a tyrant on some of us, robbing us of the bliss that is our birthright: Man was meant to live like a songbird, unfettered, free. Alas, man finds himself cribbed, cabined, and confined. He has become like a bird in a cage – he is trapped in the cage of self-centeredness!

Important for the seeker on the path is humility: for it sets free the swan bird of the soul, and the soul can soar into radiance and joy!

Guru Arjun Dev, in the *Sri Sukhmani Sahib*, says, 'The true *Brahmagyani* is one who lives in humility.' He immerses himself in austerity and lives a life of simplicity.

Sri Krishna, the Lord of the universe humbled Himself to become the charioteer of His dear, devoted disciple, Arjuna.

Maha Vishnu became *Parthasarathi* to demonstrate to us His *Kaushalya* – the quality of gentle, loving kindness – this we must all emulate.

In India, we have the beautiful tradition of greeting everyone we meet with folded hands and the reverential greeting: *Namaste!* It is a beautiful gesture of respect for the other person, and a spontaneous act of humility that ennobles both him who salutes and him who receives the salutation.

Once Gurudev Sadhu Vaswani was asked: What kind of persons would you like to associate with? Rich and famous, intelligent and scholarly, elite and sophisticated, or beautiful and charming? He replied with a magical smile, "My heart goes out to those who are humble. For they are pure at heart and are the loved ones." Therefore, let us learn to be humble and earn the Grace of God.

Our ancient Indian sages and poets admired humility as the greatest virtue in man. To illustrate this, they compared a great man with a bountiful tree laden with fruit, which bows down with its load of fresh fruits.

Let me warn you too, against false humility or superficial humility. I am sorry to say that people often assume false humility for a particular purpose. Thus subordinates bow and scrape before their superiors. Hypocrisy!

When the Kurukshetra war was over, Arjuna prepared to alight from his chariot. He was proud of his might and valour, which had been the chief factor in defeating the powerful *Kauravas*. Many *astras* and celestial weapons had been directed against him! But he had bravely stood his ground against them. They could not even touch him! Now it was time to leave the battleground, and rest his weary limbs. Before he alighted, Arjuna said to Sri Krishna, "Please alight now, Lord. You must be tired too!"

"After you, Arjuna," said Sri Krishna with a smile. "I am your *sarathi*. How can the driver alight before his passenger does? You must be the first to get off."

Delighted by the Lord's gracious reply, Arjuna descended from the chariot and prepared to hold the reins of the horses, so that Sri Krishna could alight. But to his surprise, Sri Krishna asked him to go away, and stand at a distance.

When Arjuna was at a safe distance, Sri Krishna alighted from the chariot. In a moment, the chariot was blown to pieces, disintegrating before their very eyes!

Arjuna realised that what had kept him alive and prevented his chariot from utter destruction was not his valour, but the Lord's presence. It was Sri Krishna's grace and power that had stopped all the celestial weapons hurled at Arjuna.

If the Lord had alighted from the chariot first, Arjuna would have been blown to bits without His divine protection. This was why Sri Krishna had asked him to walk away before He Himself alighted from the chariot, thus making it defenseless and submitting to the power of the various *astras* hurled against it!

Humility is not weakness: I regard it as a truly powerful weapon that can break the tyranny of the ego!

May I share with you a few simple suggestions in this regard?

- When in the midst of friends or strangers, refrain from pushing yourself forward.

- Refrain from too much talk. The less you talk, the less you will be noticed. If only we could remain silent and let others talk, it would do us a world of good.

- Always keep clear of the desire of telling others of your life and achievements, your inner struggles and experiences, your opinions and aspirations.

Remember – your real value lies not in your outer, empirical self, but in your inner, imperishable self; cultivate friendship with this inner self. And meditate on the significant words of the Gita:

> He who hath conquered
>
> His lower self of cravings and desires,
>
> He hath his Supreme Friend found
>
> In the Self, immortal, true!
>
> But he who still a victim is
>
> To his appetites and passions,
>
> Verily, the Self becometh to him,
>
> Hostile as an enemy!

The ego is a thief; the ego is our most dangerous enemy; it is the force that separates the soul from God. It is the impenetrable wall which hides us from the light with dark shadows of 'I', 'Me' and 'Mine' falling on us, obstructing our vision. When the ego goes, the Light of God glows.

SEVENTH GATEWAY:
LET SERVICE BE YOUR BADGE

Gurudev Sadhu Vaswani, was once asked, "What is your religion?" His reply was truly significant. He said, "I know of no religion higher than the religion of unity and love, of service and sacrifice."

For him, to live was to serve, to live was to love, to live was to bear the burdens of others, to live was to share his all with all.

One evening, while taking a walk with Gurudev Sadhu Vaswani

we saw a poor man lying underneath a tree. His clothes were tattered and torn; his feet were covered with mud. Gurudev stopped, he asked for a bucket of water and with his own hands he cleansed the body of the poor beggar and passed on to him his own shirt to wear! The poor man pointed to the cap on Gurudev's head, and without the least hesitation, the Master passed on the cap to him. On that occasion he spoke certain words, which I can never, ever forget. He said, "This shirt and this cap and everything that I have, is a loan given to me to be passed on to those whose need is greater than mine."

Mark the word *loan* – everything that we have is a loan given to us, to be passed on to those whose need is greater than ours. Nothing belongs to us; nothing has been given to us absolutely.

Service is the rent we have to pay for being tenants of this body.

Every morning, we must ask ourselves this question: What can I do to help, what can I do to make a difference? As Herschell Hobbs says, "The world measures a man's greatness by the number who serve him. Heaven's yardstick measures a man by the number who are served by him."

We are all born with the spirit of caring and sharing; we need to keep that spirit alive.

A great man was asked, "What are the three most important things in the life of a human being?" He answered, "The first is to care, the second is to care, the third is to care."

A Chinese proverb tells us: "If you want to be happy for an hour, take a nap. If you want to be happy for a day, go out for a picnic. If you want to be happy for a month, get married. If you want to be happy for a year, inherit a fortune. And if you want to be happy for a lifetime, go out and serve others."

Serve others – for life is too short; so let us be quick to love and prompt to serve.

We all start off by doing our duty towards our near and dear ones. This purifies our inner instrument. But we should not stop there. We belong to a larger family – to the community, to the society, to the nation, to humanity at large, to creation in all its variety and splendour!

How may we cultivate the spirit of selfless service? Let me offer you a few practical leads:

1. **Serve Silently**

   The very first rule of service is: Serve Silently! Do not serve for show or publicity. Let the right hand not know what your left hand gives away.

   There was a man who announced that he would be distributing tins of milk powder among slum dwellers. The milk powder tins were brought out, and the poor people waited eagerly to receive them – but the man would not begin the distribution. "Why aren't we getting the milk powder as promised?" they wanted to know. The answer they got made no sense to them: because the photographer had not arrived!

2. **Serve Humbly**

   The second principle of service is: Serve with humility – and this is no easy task. We think that the act of giving – is an act of superiority.

   We knew a man who had served society for years together. One day he came to meet Gurudev Sadhu Vaswani and said to him, "You know how I have served the people all these years. Now I want them to vote for me and elect me to the *Lok sabha*."

Gurudev Sadhu Vaswani smiled and said to him, "My friend, the reward of service is more service!"

Let us strive to serve humbly – let us seek no reward for our service!

3. **Serve lovingly**

The third rule of service is: Serve Lovingly! Love is what the world needs most today.

True love is love-in-action; for love that does not express itself in action, does not exist at all!

4. **Serve Unconditionally**

The fourth principle of service is: Serve Unconditionally! Service should not become interference. Nor should it be with an ulterior motive. "Blessed are those who give without remembering: and take without forgetting," says a wise statement.

5. **Cultivate the Soul**

The fifth principle of service is: Cultivate the Soul! And know that you are only a tool, an instrument of God.

Gurudev Sadhu Vaswani teaches us to worship God through service.

1. Offer your service as a duty. Think not of the fruits of action.
2. Work for the welfare of the world. Serve and be ready to suffer in service of suffering humanity.
3. Work as *yagna*: an offering to God. Dedicate your life to God. Your service becomes disinterested devotion to the Lord.

DEATH IS NOT THE END

DEATH IS MAN'S FRIEND

Is death the end of all things? Does life end with the end of the physical body? If not, what happens to us after death? Where does the individual soul go? What does it do? What are heaven and hell? Answers to these and many other questions bother us all the time.

Most of us live in the fear of death. It is usually caused by the feeling that the individual has not earned his conscious immortality, which in turn increases his fear of the Unknown. Death comes as a break in the continuity of physical life, a parting from things that man has held dear; and the uncertainty of the future makes him fear it. This fear must go!

Death is a friend of man. There is a true story given by a girl whose mother was about to pass away.

"Her eyes opened; they looked straight into mine."

'I am in God's Hands now, and it is so wonderful!' As she was saying this, she seemed bathed in light.

As I stared at her, the mysterious radiance enveloped me as well. I said to her, 'Do you mean, mother, that you see God?'

And she answered, 'Yes, face to face, and it is so important that everyone knows'.

'It's so wonderful!'

"What's so wonderful? Tell me!"

"Millions and millions of people," she began slowly. 'So many millions... and all on different levels. There is light...light everywhere – so much light! Tell them, the glory of God, it is so wonderful!'

"These were the last words which mother spoke. Her eyes closed, but the smile did not fade."

This is only one example that proves that the state of death is painless and wonderful.

Everything happens according to the Great Cosmic Will of God – including death. God is concerned and loves each one of us. And there is good in everything He plans for us and our evolution.

Man here is a traveller. The facts that man's days are numbered require him to awaken out of his dreamy slumber and recognise the power of his being and the limitlessness of his self. Everyone will bid adieu to their loved ones, their properties and possessions, the institutions they have founded and nourished with the love of their heart – man will eventually quit the scenes of life.

Farid was a great saint of Multan. He has left a number of wonderful *slokas* which still are sung in many homes. In one of his *slokas*, he says:

"O Farid! Your father and your elder brother have already passed on! Soon, your turn will come! The children that are left behind – they, too, will have to move on to the other shore!"

No one has stayed on the earth forever. No one can stay on the earth forever. Leaving the earth is what we call death, even as coming to the earth is called birth. Death is a natural phenomenon. For whosoever is born must surely die. Why, then, are we afraid of death?

We are told that the state of death is utterly painless. Before death, a man might have passed through a serious illness, on account of which his body might have experienced great physical pain: but in the few moments before death occurs, all pain ceases, and man has the most pleasant of sensations that he has ever experienced. We are also told that, after death, man continues to be what he was before death. Man remains unchanged. All his characteristics – his thoughts, his emotions, his desires, his memories – are the same; they are unchanged.

In death, man drops the physical body and continues to live in the astral body.

Do not weep, do not shed tears, do not grieve over the passing away of your dear ones, for they are not dead! They live in the life that is undying!

We must not cling to them, but we must release them, so that in their new journey, they may move on – ever onward, forward, Godward. We should remember them in our prayers and, every day, we should do some little deeds of service, in their name. This will bless them and help them in their new journey.

PREPARE FOR DEATH

Meditate on death!

In ancient India, this was the teaching that was passed on to every student. The student, in those days, was called a *jignasu*, a seeker after truth. And to the *jignasu*, the seeker after truth, the *rishi*, the teacher, said: "My child, everyday, for some time, meditate on death!" I would wish every one of you to do likewise! The day is coming when this body will drop down – the body, of which we make so much, the body of which we are proud, the body with which many of us have identified ourselves – we think we are no more than the bodies we wear – the day is coming when this body will go. Where will I be then? Where will you be then? We shall continue to exist. We have existed before our bodies were born. For we, all of us, are more ancient than the hills, more ancient than the earth on which we have built our temporary habitation. If we meditate on death, we shall no longer be afraid of death. We shall then know that death is only an illusion, death is only an appearance.

Sadhu Vaswani likened the death of the body to the sunset. He said to us: "Sunset is only an appearance, for what is sunset here is sunrise elsewhere. In reality, the sun never sets. For death here is birth elsewhere."

So let each day of our life on earth be a day of preparation.

Prepare! Prepare! This is the one word which our dear ones on the other side wish to say to us.

Prepare! Our loved ones on the "other" side see us running after money, trying to gather lakhs and crores of rupees, not a single *paisa* of which we will be allowed to carry with ourselves into the Great Beyond.

They find us running after pleasures and sense enjoyments, after name and fame, greatness and power. These are all shadows.

So they ask us to open our eyes, to wake up from the slumber of the senses and the mind and prepare for the inevitable journey.

Since life on earth is transitory, momentary, when we drop the physical body, we shall feel as though we have awakened out of a dream. Let us make the most of this life and each day prepare for our life in eternity. Here are three practical suggestions to prepare for your onward journey:

1. **Practical Suggestion number one:** Establish a link of love and devotion with God. Let us strengthen this link of love and devotion every day. Let us pray to Him, surrender ourselves to His Holy Feet, offer all our work to Him; let us, in moments of silence, converse with Him in love and with intimacy. In His presence there can be no death. For when this body drops down, He will be by us and He will lift us in His loving, everlasting arms, and He will lead us on – ever onward, ever forward, ever Godward!

2. **Practical Suggestion number two:** In the divine

providence, nothing happens but happens for our good. Remember, nothing comes a moment too soon or too late, but everything comes in its own true time. Everything that happens to us comes to bless us and lead us onward in our way. Therefore, wherever God keeps me, let me remain: wherever He sends me, let me go! Let me seek refuge at His Lotus Feet, surrendering all my problems to Him, knowing that in God is a solution to all my problems. Let me greet every happening with the words: "I accept! I accept!"

3. **Practical Suggestion number three:** How should I express it? Be a blessing to others. Those that lead selfish lives on earth, those that harm others to get little advantages for themselves, find themselves imprisoned in tiny, dark cells, when they move to the other side.

Therefore, live unselfishly. God has blessed you – with wealth and abundance, with position and power – that you may be a blessing to others. Receiving, without giving, makes a man full, proud and selfish. Give out the best in you, in God's Name, for the good of others. Lend your helping hand to those who need it. Try to lighten the loads that others carry.

As Sadhu Vaswani says the loads are not merely physical. The hearts of many are unhappy, burdened with worries and anxieties. Bring joy into the lives of those that are joyless. Give comfort to those in need of comfort. Be ready to serve, as best as you can, those that need your help and support. Never for a moment forget that life and all its bounties are given to you as a trust, to be spent in the service of the poor and needy, in the service of brother birds and animals.

GRIEVE NOT: THERE'S LIFE HEREAFTER

It is because we do not have a proper understanding of death that, when a beloved one dies, we lose our balance and are thrown into a slew of despondency, a mood of depression which lasts, in several cases, for some weeks or months. If we had a proper understanding of death, it would surely not cause us so much grief. It is true, we would miss our dear ones, who have departed, but we would know that they have not left us forever. They have but moved on to the other shore, where they await our coming.

As soon as this life ends, the next life begins.

As soon as death engulfs man, his immediate feeling is one of lightness, freedom and buoyancy. It is, as though, suddenly a burden has been lifted from his shoulders. Those that move on to the other side of death have the marvellous feeling of being free and alive.

When a man drops the physical body, he encounters a Being of Light, who may take the form of Krishna or Rama, of Buddha or Jesus, of Moses or Muhammad, of Mira or Mahavira, of Nanak or Kabir, of Zoroaster or Baha'u'llah or of some other God-man, depending on his religious background and beliefs.

When I drop the physical body, I shall encounter this Being or Form of Light. What will happen to me then? Then, every single thing that I have done, since the day I was born, will appear to me in a panoramic view. It is, as though, I shall have to witness a movie of my own life – every detail of it, every little thing that I have done either in public or in private, in light or in darkness, before the eyes of men or unseen by anyone – all the things that I have done will appear to me in a panoramic view.

I shall be filled with a feeling of remorse and repentance. My head will hang low, when all those things will appear to me, as in a movie. And they will be seen by the Being of Light, standing by my side.

I will, at the same time, have another wonderful feeling. I will feel that in the presence of the Being of Light – in the presence of Krishna or Buddha or Jesus – I am in the presence of total and absolute love – a Being, who though He knows everything about me, yet accepts me as I am and loves me unconditionally. For He is my one and the only friend.

Sadhu Vaswani gave us a wonderful definition of a friend. Who is a friend? "Your true friend is even he, who knows your faults and failings, your weaknesses and imperfections, and still loves you!" Such a one is Sri Krishna: such a one is Buddha: or any God-man that you invoke, day after day. Therefore, have I asked you, again and again, to cultivate friendship with such a one.

In His presence I feel as though I must simply cling to Him. I say to Him: "I shall never, never, never, leave you. Leave me not, O Beloved of my heart!" I fall down at His feet. I wash them with the tears of repentance that freely flow from my eyes.

So long as there is breath in this body, so long do we have the opportunity to fulfill the purpose for which we have been sent to this earth plane. Spend some time in silence, everyday, and ask yourselves the questions: "What am I? What is the purpose of my visit to the earth plane? Whither am I moving? Am I drifting away or am I drawing nearer to the goal?"

THE ASTRAL WORLD

In the book, *Life after Life*, by Raymond Moody, it is mentioned that a number of people who were declared clinically dead, came back to life after some time. What happens in such cases is that the etheric double leaves the physical body and the body becomes inert, dead: but the silver cord is not broken.

After some time, the etheric double enters the physical body via the silver cord, and the body begins to live again!

The etheric double is built up of very fine matter, etheric matter: and the etheric body has the same form as that of the physical body. Therefore, it has been called the etheric double.

There are some who are gifted with psychic sight: they have the power of clairvoyance. At the time of a person's death, such people can see the etheric double near the dying man's physical body, and they tell us that the etheric double has the same form as that of the physical body.

What is the function of the etheric double? Why do we have this body at all? It is through the etheric double that vitality flows into the physical body and keeps it alive and healthy. That which gives vitality is, in our ancient Sanskrit language, called *prana* or breath. *Prana*, or the vital force, is absorbed by the etheric double through its specialised equipment, and is despatched to every part, every cell of the physical body.

It is *prana* that makes the eyes to see and the ears to hear and the hands and feet to move. It is *prana* that makes every organ do its work. So long as the etheric double is in the physical body, the physical body can breathe and live. The moment the etheric double leaves the physical body, it drops down, becomes inert, dead.

The etheric double is connected with the physical body by means of a psychic link, which is called "the silver cord." The moment the etheric double leaves the physical body, the physical body drops down dead, but if the silver cord is intact, there is a possibility that the etheric double will once again enter the physical body via the silver cord, and the physical body will come to life.

This is what happens when we see people who were declared clinically dead, miraculously coming back to life, as I referred to above.

Those that can meditate deeply, hear the music of the silver cord. In meditation, a person gets out-of-the body experiences. Every time that the soul leaves the body and goes to higher regions, the silver cord is struck, and its music is heard. The oftener this happens, the richer is the music of the silver cord. In out-of-the-body experiences, the soul leaves the body, but the soul returns to the body. In a sense, every such experience is death, and the great masters teach their disciples to die several times every day. It is only through dying that a man learns the art of true living. The man, who has not died, will not know how to live aright.

On giving up the etheric double, at the time of death, the soul enters the astral world. The transition into the astral world should be swift and, normally, man must not linger in the etheric double. However, this is not true in the case of those who cling to matter and material objects. Such individuals continue to live in the etheric double, for it is through the etheric double that they can be in contact with the earth and earthly objects.

In the astral world, you also go through a process of disentanglement from desires and feelings. In the moment of death, everyone carries with himself certain desires and feelings. The less the number of desires, the shorter is the period of stay in the astral world. Reduce your desires to a minimum. Live a life of simplicity and purity. The man, who has learnt to control his desires, while on the earth, does not have to stay for a long period in the astral world.

The astral world is a vast region. Even as on the earth plane, there are, on the one hand, palaces and beautiful mansions, and on the other, are dirty slums, even so in the astral world, there are different sections. Each man finds his own place in the astral world. The utterly coarsened creature, selfish, cruel, malignant, will find himself, after death, in the lowest and densest regions of the astral world, surrounded by creations of his own desires and cravings.

The man, who has lived the right type of life on earth, who has always aspired to the true, the good, the beautiful, who has lived a life of service and sacrifice, of love and compassion, will find himself, after death, in lovely beautiful regions in the astral world.

The astral world is an infinite world. There is level upon levels in this world. A soul is free to go where it will; it can ascend to higher levels: it can descend to lower levels. No passports are needed: no visas are required to enter higher or lower regions of the astral world. But what happens is this: when a soul goes to a higher region, it finds itself vibrating to a higher frequency. It finds it too bright: and the light hurts its eyes. The vibrations are so refined that it cannot respond to them. It feels choked. It has a feeling of suffocation. It cannot stay there. Back must it return to the level to which it belongs, where the vibrations are in tune with its own. This is how each soul finds its own place in the astral world.

Each man finds his own place, following the law of vibrations. Therefore, during your brief sojourn on earth, make your vibrations more and more refined. The greater the frequency of your vibrations, the higher is your place in the astral world.

Here, you will find yourself surrounded by like-minded people. Since each person thinks in his own way and has independent views, you will have a lot to learn from them in whose company you find yourself.

In the astral world, you make the great discovery that thought is all-powerful. Whatever the mind thinks of is immediately created. Therefore, we must learn to control our thoughts.

Movement in the astral world is swift, as quick as lightning. Howsoever far a person may move, he does not feel tired. Fatigue is unknown to the astral body. The astral body does not need to sleep, for it does not exist – except, of course, if you think of a particular disease, you will immediately feel that you have fallen sick.

TREASURES UNPERISHABLE

Every day, we think of what will happen to us when we move on to the other side of death. We shall encounter the Being of Light. We shall come face to face, with the Beloved of our hearts – with Krishna, Buddha and Jesus and He will put to us the question: "My child, what have you done with your life?"

So let us ask ourselves now, while we are alive: What are we doing with our life?

While it is necessary to work and earn one's livelihood, one must not neglect the Treasure Imperishable. These are the treasures which thieves cannot steal, waters cannot wet, and the winds cannot dry and moths cannot corrupt.

Every day, let us try to gather a little of this treasure. Therefore, pray, meditate, spend some time in silence. Do *swadhyay* – self-study. Put to yourself the questions: What am I here for? What is the purpose of my visit to this earth plane? Whither am I moving? Am I drifting away or am I drawing closer to the goal?

Every day, spend some time in silence and sing the Name of God, seek the company of the pure, the wise and the holy. Everyday do little acts of service to the poor and broken ones, to brother birds and animals. Do them in love of God. For the poor, as Sadhu Vaswani said, are the pictures of God.

We must not linger in the etheric double. Our passage through the etheric double must be swift and instantaneous.

Never regard anything as your own. How often have I not meditated on the *sloka* of the great guru:

Tudh aagay ardass hamaari, jeeya pinda sabh tera,
Kaho Nanak sabh teri vadiyai, koi naun na jaanay mera!

"*Jeeya*" or "*Jiva*" is the animate principle, the principle of life. "*Jiva*" is what we call the soul, the spirit. And "*pinda*" is matter, the physical body, the inanimate principle. Matter and life both, the body and the spirit belong to Thee, O Lord! Nothing belongs to me. No one belongs to me.

Learn self-control. Develop self-discipline. It is desires that lead man astray. Desire is man's deadly foe. There are specially three types of desires against which each one of us must guard.

There is, firstly, the desire for money, greed of gold, which makes a man commit the vilest crimes.

Then there is the desire, in the second place, for power, the lust for power. And as Lord Acton has said: "Power corrupts, and absolute power corrupts absolutely!"

There is, thirdly, the desire for sense gratification, the desire for sense enjoyment, sense pleasure. These desires – what a procession they make – a tumultuous procession, bewildering man, leading him from darkness to darkness. Therefore, learn self-control. Develop self-discipline. Learn the lesson of abstinence.

Abstain from all unholy, impure desires. Therefore, be vigilant at all the times. Every time you are disturbed by desire, withdraw into the self within you – the true self which no desire can touch.

At the close of this chapter, may I pass on to you a few practical suggestions for making your after life better!

1. **Practical suggestion number one:**

    Repent for all the sins of omission and commission of the day. Repentance brings about a change of heart. Out of the heart are the issues of life. When the heart changes, man becomes new. He longs to dedicate his life to God. Man becomes a child of God. He becomes innocent as a child. Innocence is far better than penitence.

    Sadhu Vaswani said "There is a treasure God giveth in darkness, and sinners are nearer the kingdom of Love than the self-righteous."

    So be not depressed! But trust in the law of love and worship the One you seek with flowers of anguished aspiration. Ask God to forgive you for your sins, your misdeeds, and ask Him to give you the strength to become new.

2. **Ask for forgiveness**– yes. But do not forget that before you ask for forgiveness, you must forgive those that have wronged you. Jesus taught a beautiful prayer to his disciples. In the prayer are the following words:

    "Forgive us our trespasses, even as we forgive those that trespass against us!"

    Learn to forgive even before forgiveness is asked. And let our forgiveness be liberal. There are some people whose forgiveness is so miserly that they will never let you forget that they have forgiven you at all. Let our forgiveness be generous and rich, making us forget completely the wrong that has been done to us.

3. While on earth, let us learn the language of the astral world: It is the language of love – pure, passionless, selfless love. In every thought, in every word, in every deed, let us

express the pure, unselfish love of our heart.

To love is to serve, to love is to give, to love is to go out of one's way to bring comfort to another, to love is to sacrifice everything for the sake of those that suffer and are in pain.

THE MYTH OF HEAVEN AND HELL

What is Heaven? And what is Hell? I believe there is no place called Hell. Theologians frighten us with the thought that the sinner is doomed to eternal punishment, that the sinner must burn eternally in the fires of hell. Nothing is farther from the truth.

God is pure love, compassion and wisdom. Indeed, God is love. Love is not an attribute of God; Love is not a quality of God. Love is God and God is Love. Love cannot bear to see anyone suffer. Love would wish each one of us to grow in purity and unselfishness. Therefore, if there are any fires, they are chastening fires, purifying fires. The moment a soul is sufficiently purified; he need not be in the fire.

There is no hell, but we may say that there is purgatory, a sort of a psychic quarantine, where some souls are required to remain for some time to be cleansed, washed, purified, before they proceed in their onward march. There is no idea of punishment behind the purgatory.

In purgatory, the soul is forced to face its own record. All the sins of omission and commission that a person has committed during his sojourn on earth, stand before him. When the soul faces his own record, he reacts to it.

Purgatory is simply the forced realisation of the significance of our own misdeeds. No one catches hold of us and drags us to purgatory. Heaven and hell or purgatory are not places, but states of consciousness.

In purgatory, the soul is purified, even as gold is tried in the crucible, until all its dross is burnt away. The soul thereby wipes out only a part of his karma and, in due course, comes back to the earth with the rest still clinging to him, and it is this unexpiated karma that causes him to suffer in the next life.

What is the heaven world? If the purgatory is a hospital for the healing of sick souls, going to the heaven world is like visiting a hill station. There is so much of beauty and peace there.

In the heaven world, our unfulfilled desires of a higher nature find expression. Heaven is a world of wish fulfilment. Each one of us has a number of wishes of a higher type, which for some reason or the other, we are unable to fulfil during the period of our stay on earth. Those wishes are fulfilled in heaven.

In the heaven world there is no rain; if you want rain, all you have to do is to think of rain and the rain will begin to pour. But, mind you, it will be your private rain. It is only you, who will feel it. The person next to you will not feel it at all, unless he too wishes for rain.

There is, however, only one limitation. It is a self-imposed limitation and depends upon a man's desire and habits, the emotional patterns he is used to during his life on earth. To give you an illustration, take the case of an individual, who has been hobbling about on crutches for many years, prior to the death of his physical body. The idea of hobbling about on crutches has been firmly fixed in his mind. When he enters the astral body, he has not shaken off this fixed idea and he continues to think of himself as a cripple and hobbles about on astral crutches. He will repeatedly need to be told: "Brother, you no longer need those crutches. For here in the astral world, you don't even have to walk to get where you are going." In the astral world, if you have to reach a particular place – however far it may be in matter of earthly distance, the place may be thousands of miles away – all you have to do is visualise clearly where you have to reach. You have only to wish – and you are there.

Therefore, do not identify yourselves with the bodies that you wear. You are not the body that you have put on. You are ever free. It is the body that falls sick: you do not fall sick. It is the body that is crippled: you can never be a cripple.

In the heaven world, the soul keeps on rising higher and higher, until the last earthly ties are dissolved and all links with the world's sorrow and pain are ended. Then, once again, the soul enters into sleep. It is a deep, serene sleep. This is the death of the astral body. The first is the death of the physical body. The second is the death of the astral body. From this sleep the soul awakes in a new world. How shall I name it? For want of a better name, it has been called, the world of the Gods. In this new world – the world of the Gods – man can carry with himself only selfless love and other elements of his higher nature – all that he has expressed on earth of the good, the true, the beautiful and the holy. The period of stay in the World of Gods is truly a blissful period of rest and refreshment. He realises that he is a God. *Tat twam asi!* That art thou! This and other deep realisations dawn on the soul in this new world. You will be surprised if I tell you that many of the experiences through which you are passing today – the so-called misfortunes, sickness of the body, accidents, financial crises and other happenings, were determined by you while you dwelt in the tranquil atmosphere of the world of Gods. There you gathered that the so-called misfortunes were necessary for the progress of your soul, the unfolding of your *atmic shakti*. Coming here, you have forgotten that you yourself wrote down your destiny, and you seek to escape that which is for your ultimate good. Therefore, the law of life is acceptance. Accept everything that happens to you, knowing that there is some hidden good in every incident and accident of life. Every bitter experience of life has some hidden good in it. Therefore, rejoice in all that happens and move on – ever onward, forward, Godward. We are not alone in the afterlife. So many of our dear ones, who have already passed on, will bear us company. In their company, we shall easily forget our earthly attachments. Therefore, do not live in fear of death. In the journey beyond death, you will not be alone.

REACHING OUT TO OUR LOVED ONES ON THE OTHER SIDE

Is it alright to communicate with the dead?

The answer to this is that as long as it is done within limits, it is alright.

There are many who, at the death of their dear ones, feel disconsolate and want an assurance that their dear departed continue to live in the astral world and are happy. For these people, it is alright if they communicate with the dead and get the assurance they need. But beyond this, they must not go. For calling back the dead, repeatedly, disturbs them in the new world to which they have moved and prevents them from settling down to their new conditions.

THE BEST WAY TO DIE

There are two types of death. There is the peaceful or natural way of dying: and there is the unpeaceful or unnatural way of dying. The best way to die is to die a natural death. This occurs in a variety of ways.

1. Old age
2. Another natural form of death is what is called cerebral

hemorrhage.

3. There is yet a third natural form of death. As the years roll on, the heart gradually becomes weaker, until it finally stops at the hour of lowest vitality, usually the small hours of the night. In such cases, the person dies in his sleep.

All these are natural forms of death and are the ones to be desired. But the best form of death is that in which a man dies with his mind fixed on the Lord, his heart filled with holy love, and his lips uttering the Name Divine!

In the case of a man, who dies in an accident, the soul, as it were, is suddenly pushed out of the body. Because death has come so quickly, it is dazed. For some time, the soul may not even realise that it has been separated from the physical body. In the astral world, as I said on an earlier occasion, there are a number of service groups. Some of the service groups are charged with the task of attending to such souls who are suddenly ejected from their physical bodies. These helpers hover like hawks in the astral world, watching for incoming souls who are in need of help. Immediately they rush to their aid and help them to adjust to new conditions.

In several cases, those that die in accidents soon reincarnate, to complete the work of their earlier incarnation. But if a person who dies in an accident has lived a reasonably good, pure life, devoted to the service of his fellow beings, such a soul need not reincarnate immediately. Such a soul goes at once into a state of quiet, harmonious sleep, out of which he awakens in higher astral or heaven world, the vibrations of which are in tune with his own.

What of people who undergo the death penalty and die at the gallows?

Such people are ejected, against their will, from the physical world. They do not want to die but are forcibly dragged to the death chamber. In their last moments, their hearts are usually filled with feelings of fear, horror and hatred and, not often, with a violent thirst for revenge.

There are some innocent persons who, due to an error of judgement or otherwise, are condemned to capital punishment. There are others – patriots who, for no fault of theirs, are condemned to die on the gallows, by a cruel, despotic government.

Those who are unjustly condemned to capital punishment should bear the misfortune patiently, knowing that there is a law which is infallible, a law which can never err, a law which, for our own benefit, gives us the fruits of our acts, whether they were committed in this or earlier lives. This law, the rishis of ancient India called, the Law of Karma. This law is not punitive: it is essentially reformative.

In the moment of death, let there be no hatred, no resentment, no desire for revenge. Let the heart be infused with feelings of love – love for those that love us and for those who are unable to love us.

The person, who commits suicide, becomes, immediately, after death, an earthbound spirit. He feels unhappier and restless after suicide than when he was in the physical body. The misery, the sorrow, the anguish, from which he thought he could escape by committing suicide, have been aggravated. His agony has increased. The man who commits suicide finds that, instead of solving his problems, the suicide has only intensified its worst features. He feels that it would have been far better if, instead of committing suicide, he had slept over it and reconsidered the situation, the next morning, or sought help and advice from a spiritual elder, or prayed to the Lord for guidance. Life is given us by God: it is only He who can take it away. If we take the law in our own hands, we have to pay a heavy price for it.

Can we do anything to help the man who has committed suicide?

Yes – we can do much to help the person who has committed suicide and is now become an earthbound spirit.

Through the power of meditation, the rays of love divine can be sent to the unfortunate one so that they surround him and give rest to his restless soul, and wake up within him his own spiritual powers which alone can free him from his self-imposed shackles.

CAN ASTROLOGY PREDICT DEATH?

Astrology is more of an art than a science, and much depends upon the astrologer who prepared your horoscope and the one who reads it.

In every horoscope there are periods when death is likely to occur. And if you are forewarned, you can be very careful and so can avoid death. I have known cases in which the faith and will power of the person concerned, or someone close to him, have helped the person to tide over the crisis. Once the period is crossed over, conditions become normal, until another such period enters your life.

In the end neither birth nor death is in our hands. It is in the hands of the Lord. Ours is to live this life in the best way we can and make the most of it by a life of gratitude and His praise.

NIRVANA

Men are born, they live their allotted span of life, then die, pass through the etheric double, move on to the astral world, where they keep on ascending higher and higher until, purified of all dross, they enter the world of the Gods. Then they return and, in their return journey, they pick up a new astral body and are reborn in the physical world, wearing a new physical body. And the process goes on. Is there no way out?

There is a way out. There are two paths. There is, firstly, the path of bondage and return to rebirth. There is, secondly, the path of light and liberation, emancipation, freedom from the cycle of birth and death.

In the first path, the path of bondage and rebirth, move many of us. What keeps us in bondage, what binds us to the cycle of birth and death is desire. Each one of us has desires. Our desires are the chains with which we bind ourselves to the wheel of birth and death. We work with a desire for fruit: we act with a desire for reward. No one, today, is prepared to work without getting something for his work.

There are some who work, but want nothing for themselves in this world: they desire to earn heaven. This desire, too, binds us to the wheel. So, after death, we move on from sphere to sphere, we enjoy the fruits of our good actions, and when the merit of our good deeds is exhausted, back must we return to this mortal world.

There is, however, another path – the path of light and liberation. It is trodden by a few noble souls who, having passed through a cycle of experiences, have grown in purity and unselfishness, love and compassion, devotion and spirituality. They desire nothing – not even the joys of the heaven world. They work and their work is an oblation to the Lord, at the altar of suffering creation.

They want nothing for themselves. They regard themselves as

broken instruments in the hands of the Lord. "All glory be unto Thee," they exclaim with every breath of their being! "Not mine, but Thine be the glory, O Lord!" They desire nothing.

As they have no desire, there is nothing that can bind them to the wheel of birth and death. After the death of the physical body, they move on the path of light and reach the abode of the highest, from where none returneth. It is the abode of *Brahman*, the *Brahmanloka*. It is the abode of the Eternal.

Books and Booklets by J.P. Vaswani

In English:

7 Commandments of the Bhagavad Gita
10 Commandments of a Successful Marriage
108 Pearls of Practical Wisdom
108 Simple Prayers of a Simple Man
108 Thoughts on Success
114 Thoughts on Love
A Little Book of Life
A Little Book of Wisdom
A Love that is Love Indeed!
A Simple and Easy Way to God
A Treasure of Quotes - Vol. I
A Treasure of Quotes - Vol. II
Alphabets of Good Life
Around the Camp Fire
Be An Achiever
Be in the Driver's Seat
Begin the Day With God
Bhagavad Gita in a Nutshell
Burn Anger Before Anger Burns You
Comrades of God— Lives of Saints From East & West
Daily Appointment With God
Daily Inspiration (A Thought for Every Day of the Year)
Daily Inspiration
Dashavatara
Destination Happiness
Dewdrops of Love
Does God Have Favourites?
Ego Goes: Divinity Grows
Empower Yourself
Enrich Your Life - Desk Calendar
Face it With Love
Finding Peace of Mind
Formula for Prosperity
Friends Forever
From Hell to Heaven
Gateways to Heaven
God in Quest of Man
Good Parenting
Happily Ever After
How to Overcome Depression
I am a Sindhi
I Luv U, God!
India Awake
Jap Sahib - An Interpretation
Joy Peace Pills
Kill Fear Before Fear Kills You
Ladder of Abhyasa
Lessons Life Has Taught Me
Life After Death
Life and Teachings of Sadhu Vaswani
Life and Teachings of the Sikh Gurus: Ten Companions of God
Living in the Now
Make the Right Choice
Management Moment by Moment
Mantra for the Modern Man
Mantras for Peace of Mind
Many Paths: One Goal
Many Scriptures: One Wisdom
Moment of Calm - Desk Calendar
Nearer, My God, to Thee!
New Education Can Make the World New
Peace or Perish
Practise the Presence of God
Positive Power of Thanksgiving
Questions Answered
Rainbow of Love
Saints for You and Me
Saints With a Difference
Say No to Negatives
Secrets of Health and Happiness
Seven Steps on the Path
Shake Hands With Life
Short Sketches of Saints Known & Unknown
Sketches of Saints Known & Unknown
Spirituality in Daily Life
Stay Connected

Stop Complaining: Start Thanking!
Swallow Irritation Before Irritation Swallows You
Switch on the Light
Teachers are Sculptors
The Endless Quest
The Goal of Life and How to Attain it
The Highway to Happiness
The Little Book of Freedom From Stress
The Little Book of Prayer
The Little Book of Service
The Little Book of Success
The Little Book of Yoga
The Magic of Forgiveness
The New Age Diet: Vegetarianism for You and Me
The Perfect Relationship: Guru and Disciple
The Simple Way
The Terror Within
The Way of Abhyasa (How to Meditate)
Thus Have I Been Taught
Tips for Teenagers
What Then?
What You Would Like to Know About Karma
What You Would Like to Know About Hinduism
What to Do When Difficulties Strike
Why Do Good People Suffer?
Why Be Sad?
Women: Where Would the World be Without You?
You Are Not Alone: God is With You!
You Can Change Your Life: Live—Don't Just Exist!

Story Books:
100 Stories You Will Never Forget
100 Love Stories That Will Touch Your Heart
101 Stories for You and Me
25 Stories for Children and also for Teens
It's All a Matter of Attitude
Immortal Stories: Wisdom to Nourish Your Mind & Soul
Snacks for the Soul
More Snacks for the Soul
Stories With a Difference From the Bhagavata Purana
Break the Habit
The King of Kings
The One Thing Needful
The Patience of Purna
The Power of Good Deeds
The Power of Thought
The Miracle of Forgiving
Trust Me All in All or Not at All
Whom Do You Love the Most?
You Can Make a Difference

In Hindi:
Aadarsh Jeevan Ki Prerak Kahaniyaan
Aalwar Santon Ki Mahan Gaathaayen
Aapkay Karm, Aapkaa Bhaagya Banaatay Hein
Achche Mata Pita Kaise Bane
Atmik Jalpaan
Atmik Poshan
Bhakton Ki Uljhanon Kaa Saral Upaai
Bhale Logon Ke Saath Bura Kyon?
Chaahat Hai Mujhe Ik Teri Teri
Dainik Prerna
Dar Se Mukti Paayen
Ishwar Tujhe Pranam
Khushaal Jeevan Ki Kahaniyaan
Krodh Ko Jalayen Swayam Ko Nahin
Laghu Kathayein
Mrityu Hai Dwar… Phir Kya?
Na Bhoolnewali 100 Kahaniyaan
Prarthana ki Shakti

Shama Karne Ki Aloukik Shakti
Sadhu Vaswani: Unkaa Jeevan Aur
  Shikshaayen
Safal Vivah Ke Dus Rahasya
Santon Ki Leela
Sarvottam Sambandh
Shama Karo Sukhi Raho
Srimad Bhagavad Gita: Gaagar Mein
  Saagar

In Arabic:
Daily Appointment With God
Daily Inspiration

In Bahasa:
A Little Book of Success
A Little Book of Wisdom
Burn Anger Before Anger Burns You
It's All a Matter of Attitude
Life After Death

In Chinese:
Daily Appointment With God

In Dutch:
Begin the Day With God
Women: Where Would the World be
  Without You?

In French:
Burn Anger Before Anger Burns You

In German:
Secrets of Health and Happiness

In Gujarati:
Daily Appointment With God
Flowers & Fruits
It's All a Matter of Attitude
Life After Death

In Kannada:
101 Stories for You and Me
Burn Anger Before Anger Burns You
Dada Answers

Life After Death
Tips for Teenagers
Why do Good People Suffer?

In Konkani:
Be in the Driver's Seat

In Letvian:
The Magic of Forgiveness

In Marathi:
10 Commandments of a Successful
  Marriage
101 Stories for You and Me
Burn Anger Before Anger Burns You
Life After Death
Management Moment by Moment
Questions Answered
Sadhu Vaswani: His Life and
  Teachings
Shake Hands With Life
Spirituality in Daily Life
Switch on the Light
The Little Book of Prayer
The Magic of Forgiveness
What You Would Like to Know
  About Karma

In Oriya:
Be in the Driver's Seat
Burn Anger Before Anger Burns You
Empower Yourself
Kill Fear Before Fear Kills You
Life After Death
More Snacks for the Soul
Snacks for the Soul
The Little Book of Prayer
Why Do Good People Suffer?

In Punjabi:
Burn Anger Before Anger Burns You

In Romanian:
Daily Inspiration (A Thought for
  Every Day of the Year)

In Russian:
Burn Anger Before Anger Burns You
What You Would Like to Know
    About Karma

In Sindhi:
Anjali Sangraha
Bhagavad Gita in a Nutshell
Bhaj Gobindam
Burn Anger Before Anger Burns You
Life After Death
Why Do Good People Suffer?

In Spanish:
10 Commandments of a Successful
    Marriage
101 Stories for You and Me
Begin the Day With God
Be In The Driver's Seat
Burn Anger Before Anger Burns You
Dada Answers
Daily Appointment With God
Daily Inspiration
Does God Have Favourites?
Formula for Prosperity
Good Parenting
I Luv U, God!
It's All a Matter of Attitude
Kill Fear Before Fear Kills You
Life After Death
Management Moment by Moment
More Dada Answers
More Snacks for the Soul
Nearer My God to Thee
Positive Power of Thanksgiving
Say No to Negatives
Shake Hands With Life
Snacks for the Soul
Stop Complaining Start Thanking
Spirituality in Daily Life
Swallow Irritation Before Irritation
    Swallows You
The Good You Do Returns
The Miracle of Forgiving
Thus have I Been Taught

What to do when Difficulties Strike
What You Would Like to Know
    About Karma
You Can Make a Difference

In Tamil:
10 Commandments of a Successful
    Marriage
Burn Anger Before Anger Burns You
Daily Appointment With God
It's All a Matter of Attitude
Kill Fear Before Fear Kills You
More Snacks for the Soul
Secrets of Health and Happiness
Snacks for the Soul
Why Do Good People Suffer?
You Can Make a Difference

In Telugu:
What You Would Like to Know
    About Karma

In Urdu:
Begin the Day With God
Steps to Happiness
Ticket to Heaven

In Vietnamese:
It's All a Matter of Attitude

Other Publications:
Books on J. P. Vaswani:
Dada J. P. Vaswani's Historic Visit
    to Sind
Dost Thou Keep Memory
How to Embrace Pain
Interviews and Innerviews
Jadhein Pireen Karay Tho Pandh
Jiski Jholi Mein Hai Pyaar
Dada J. P. Vaswani His Life and
    Teachings
Living Legend
Moments With a Master
Munhinjee Dil Te Lagee
    Laahootiyun Saan

Pyar Ka Masiha
Pilgrim of Love
Conversations With Dada Vaswani:
    A Perfect Disciple, A Reluctant
    Master
Guru of None, Disciple of All– The
    Life & Times of Dada J. P.
    Vaswani
Dada Vaswani: A Life in Spirituality
To Know Him... Is to Love Him!
Kadir and the Magical Lighthouse
A Messenger of Love